Public Speaking Mastery

Practical Guide to Speak with
Confidence, Turn Fear into Fuel, Elevate
your Influence with Storytelling and
Command Any Room.

Sawsan Charif

Brain Corner Publishing

Contents

Dedication

To the fearless voices within us all,
The ones that dare to rise despite fear, doubt, and uncertainty.

To those who aspire to inspire,
Who see public speaking not as a hurdle,
But as a bridge to connection, growth, and change.

And to my students, mentors, and supporters,
Your unwavering belief in the power of communication
Has shaped this journey and made this book possible.

This is for you—the dreamers, the doers, the storytellers.
May your voice find its stage and your words leave a lasting impact.

A Special Thanks to My Students

To my amazing students,

This book wouldn't exist without you. Every lesson we shared, every challenge you overcame, and every triumph you celebrated has inspired me in ways I can't fully express. Watching you step out of your comfort zones, find your voices, and grow into confident communicators has been one of the greatest joys of my life.

Your courage and determination reminded me why I started this journey—to help people like you embrace their potential and share their unique stories with the world.

Thank you for being my inspiration and for trusting me to be a part of your journey.

Introduction

A few years ago, I stood in front of a room filled with eager faces, all waiting for me to speak. My heart raced, my palms were clammy, and doubt swirled in my mind. I was about to lead a workshop on communication skills—something I had done countless times before. Yet, the fear I felt was undeniable, almost overwhelming. In that moment, I realized a universal truth: the fear of public speaking can grip anyone, no matter how seasoned or skilled they are. But I also discovered something profound: fear isn't the enemy—it's a catalyst for growth.

This book was born from that realization. It's here to empower you, to transform that fear into confidence, and to serve as a practical guide filled with actionable strategies. Whether you're addressing a boardroom, a conference, or even a small team meeting, my goal is to equip you with the tools to speak with authority, elevate your influence, and command attention through the art of public speaking. Confidence is cultivated not just in practice but also in embracing vulnerability. Consider using affirmations, visualizing success, and reflecting on your past accomplishments as tools to boost self-assurance. These habits, when practiced consistently, create a foundation of unwavering confidence.

I know the challenges you face—the pounding anxiety before stepping on stage, the self-doubt that creeps in when facing an audience, and the struggle to keep your listeners engaged. These hurdles are universal, but they're also conquerable. With the right mindset and techniques, you can turn fear into your greatest asset.

That's where Cognitive Behavioral Therapy (CBT) comes in. By reprogramming negative thoughts, CBT offers powerful tools to reframe your perspective. It helps you transform anxiety into confidence, turning what once held you back into a driving force for success. Confidence is cultivated not just in practice but also in embracing vulnerability. Consider using affirmations, visualizing success, and reflecting on your past accomplishments as tools to boost self-assurance. These habits, when practiced consistently, create a foundation of unwavering confidence.

What sets this book apart is its unique approach, combining psychological insights with proven public speaking techniques. At the heart of this is storytelling—a timeless skill that connects you to your audience on a deeply emotional level. Storytelling isn't just about entertaining; it's about building trust, inspiring action, and creating a connection that leaves a lasting impression. Storytelling serves as the bridge between facts and emotions, allowing the audience to visualize and internalize the message. Adding a vivid description or a relatable personal anecdote can make the message even more memorable. Think of a moment when a story changed your perspective—it is this transformation that storytelling brings to public speaking.

Allow me to introduce myself. I'm Sawsan—an ESL teacher, blogger, and author dedicated to helping others find their voice. Over the years, I've worked with professionals, leaders, and learners, guiding them to overcome communication barriers and unlock their potential. I've seen the transformative power of public speaking firsthand, and my passion is helping people like you conquer their fears and achieve their goals.

Building confidence requires both practice and the courage to embrace vulnerability. Incorporating affirmations, visualizing success, and reflecting on achievements can significantly boost self-assurance.

So, what can you expect from this book? Each chapter is designed to be practical, relatable, and actionable. You'll find step-by-step techniques, real-world examples, and exercises that you can apply immediately. Every concept builds on the last, guiding you towards becoming a confident and effective communicator.

Public speaking isn't just a professional skill—it's a personal one. The tools you'll gain in these pages will serve you in every aspect of your life, from career advancements to meaningful relationships and beyond.

As we begin this journey, I want you to remember one thing: every great speaker started where you are now. They faced their fears, embraced the process, and grew into the leaders we admire today. The same transformation is within your reach. Let's embark on this adventure together. It's time to find your voice and unlock the power to inspire and lead.

Let's begin.

SPECIAL BONUS!

NAIL THE FIRST MINUTE—COMMAND ATTENTION FROM THE START!

As a **small token of thanks for buying this book**, I am offering a free bonus gift to my readers.

The first 60 seconds of your speech can make or break your impact. Are you ready to hook your audience, build instant confidence, and set the stage for a memorable presentation?

In *The First Minute Magic*, public speaking I will unveil powerful, actionable techniques to help you:

Overcome nervousness and project confidence effortlessly

Capture attention instantly with proven opening strategies

Craft a strong first impression that sets the tone for success

Engage your audience right from the start with storytelling, questions, and hooks

Whether you're a business professional, entrepreneur, educator, or leader, this practical guide will transform how you begin any presentation.

BONUS: This book is your exclusive guide to the first minute of your speech, complementing the full *Public Speaking Mastery* system.

Start strong. Speak with confidence. Make an unforgettable impact.

Get FREE unlimited access to it and all of my new books by joining my Readers Club.

Click Here to download!

or scan with your camera

Chapter One

Breaking the Ice

Standing backstage, waiting for your turn to speak, can feel like an eternity. Your heart pounds, your hands tremble, and a little voice in your head whispers doubts. If this sounds familiar, you're not alone—many professionals, even the most experienced, have faced that same daunting moment. The difference lies in how they manage and channel that anxiety. This chapter marks your first step in transforming fear into a powerful tool for growth. Together, we'll uncover the roots of speaking anxiety, help you identify your personal triggers, and equip you with practical strategies to manage them effectively.

1.1 Understanding the Roots of Speaking Anxiety

Public speaking anxiety often stems from a deep-seated fear of judgment—the idea that your peers, colleagues, or audience might critique every word you say. This fear is tied to our innate psychological need for acceptance and approval. But it's not just the fear of judgment at play. Perfectionism amplifies this anxiety, as the pressure to deliver a flawless presentation sets unattainable expectations. Add to that the weight of past negative experiences—perhaps a presentation that went poorly or a time you blanked out on stage—and it's no wonder public speaking feels so daunting. These memories can create a mental barrier, reinforcing the belief that speaking in public is fraught with risk.

Cognitive Behavioral Therapy (CBT)

Cognitive Behavioral Therapy offers valuable tools to break this cycle. CBT focuses on identifying and challenging negative thought patterns that fuel anxiety. One effective method is keeping a thought log. For instance, write down a specific fear, such as, "I'll embarrass myself." Then, counter it with evidence-based statements like, "I've practiced thoroughly and am prepared." This exercise shifts your perspective, reducing anxiety's grip on your actions. By reframing these thoughts, you can replace fear with a sense of control and preparedness, paving the way for more confident and positive speaking experiences.

Recognizing the Physical Symptoms of Anxiety

Anxiety isn't just a mental game; it manifests physically too. Sweaty palms, trembling hands, heart palpitations, and shortness of breath are all common symptoms of speaking anxiety. These physical reactions can make it challenging to project your voice and maintain composure on stage. Recognizing these signs is the first step to managing them. By understanding how anxiety shows up in your body, you can proactively develop strategies to counteract these symptoms.

Techniques like deep breathing exercises and mindfulness practices can help calm your nerves and restore your focus. Deep breathing slows your heart rate and eases physical tension, allowing you to approach the stage with a steadier mind and body. Mindfulness keeps you grounded in the present moment, helping you break free from the spiral of worry and regain control. Addressing both the physical and mental aspects of anxiety creates a holistic strategy for overcoming your fears.

The Influence of Culture and Society

Cultural and societal expectations can also heighten public speaking anxiety. In high-stakes environments—where every word might impact your career or reputation—the pressure to perform flawlessly is magnified. This is further complicated when speaking in diverse cultural contexts, where norms and expectations can vary widely. Understanding these external factors is crucial. By tailoring your approach to suit different audiences and settings, you'll feel more prepared and adaptable, which will help ease anxiety and foster better connections.

Being mindful of these dynamics also builds confidence as a speaker. Whether you're addressing a culturally diverse audience or navigating a high-pressure environment, adaptability is key to breaking through anxiety and achieving success in any speaking situation. Confidence is cultivated not just through practice but also through embracing vulnerability. Consider using affirmations, visualizing success, and reflecting on your past accomplishments as tools to boost self-assurance. These habits, when practiced consistently, create a foundation of unwavering confidence.

Managing the "Fight or Flight" Response

At its core, public speaking anxiety is tied to the body's natural "fight or flight" response. When faced with a perceived threat—like speaking in front of an audience—the brain signals the body to prepare for action. While this response is useful in true danger, it can interfere with effective communication. Racing thoughts, sweating, and trembling hands are all byproducts of this reaction.

True confidence develops through consistent practice and self-reflection. Affirmations, visualization, and recognizing past successes are powerful ways to strengthen it.

Embracing vulnerability alongside regular practice helps cultivate confidence. Techniques like visualization and affirmations reinforce self-belief and resilience.

1.2 Transforming Anxiety into Positive Energy

Public speaking often stirs a whirlwind of emotions, but what if you could view those feelings differently? Reframing anxiety as excitement is a powerful technique that transforms nerves into a source of energy. Anxiety and excitement are closely linked—they activate the same physiological responses. It's your perception that differentiates them. Successful speakers often share how they shift their narrative, viewing anxiety not as a hindrance but as an ally. This mental shift, known as cognitive restructuring, involves changing how you interpret these sensations.

Turning nervous energy into enthusiasm and engagement is not only possible but also practical. Breathing exercises are foundational tools in this transformation. Focused breathing regulates your body's stress response, calming your mind and instilling a sense of control.

Try inhaling deeply through your nose, holding for a count of three, and exhaling slowly through your mouth. This simple technique centers you and reduces tension. Pair it with physical movements to release pent-up energy—light stretches or a brisk walk can invigorate you, channeling nervousness into readiness. Think of athletes shaking out their limbs before a big game. You, too, can use similar techniques to convert anxiety into a performance enhancer.

Mindfulness practices can further ground you in the present, anchoring your thoughts and easing anxiety. Mindful breathing, for example, focuses your attention on the rhythm of your breath, silencing the mental chatter. Close your eyes, inhale deeply, and allow yourself to fully experience each breath. Another effective tool is the body scan exercise: mentally scan from head to toe, identifying and consciously releasing areas of tension. These practices not only calm your nerves but also increase awareness of how anxiety manifests physically, empowering you to manage it effectively.

These techniques transform anxiety into a source of positive energy. By reframing your perception and applying practical strategies, you can turn a daunting prospect into an exhilarating opportunity. Remember, anxiety is your signal that you're ready—it's your cue to step forward and deliver with confidence and passion. With practice, you'll channel nervous energy into powerful performances, connecting with your audience and communicating effectively. Confidence is cultivated not just in practice but also in embracing vulnerability. Consider using affirmations, visualizing success, and reflecting on your past accomplishments as tools to boost self-assurance. Regularly applying these strategies builds a strong and lasting sense of confidence.

1.3 Incremental Exposure:

Confidence in public speaking doesn't happen overnight—it's a process of **gradual exposure and consistent practice**. Think of it like **learning to swim**: you don't dive into the deep end right away; you start by dipping your toes, getting comfortable, and progressively taking on bigger challenges.

A great way to **ease into public speaking** is by practicing in **low-pressure environments**. Start small—speak up in team meetings, present ideas to a close group of friends, or participate in a local discussion group. These settings allow you to **build confidence** in a **supportive atmosphere** where mistakes are learning opportunities. As you gain comfort, **increase the difficulty level** by presenting to **larger groups**, leading professional meetings, or speaking at formal events. This step-by-step approach helps you acclimate to the spotlight **without feeling overwhelmed**.

Setting Milestones for Growth

Rather than expecting immediate mastery, set **realistic milestones** to track your progress. For example:

- Delivering a short talk without relying on notes

- Making eye contact with multiple audience members

- Engaging the audience with a question or story

Every small win adds up, reinforcing **your confidence and skill set**. Keeping a journal to reflect on what **worked well** and where you can improve will help you **identify patterns** and adjust your approach accordingly.

Simulated Practice: Role-Playing & VR Tools

Another great way to **refine your public speaking skills** is through **simulated practice**.

Role-playing in workshops or practice groups can prepare you for real-world situations, helping you fine-tune delivery and handle unexpected scenarios.

Virtual Reality (VR) tools now offer immersive simulations where you can practice **speaking in front of virtual audiences**, replicating the experience **without real-world pressure**.

By incorporating **incremental exposure**, setting **achievable goals**, and practicing in **controlled environments**, you will steadily build the confidence to **command any stage with ease**.

1.4 Visualization Techniques for Calming Nerves

Visualization is a powerful tool that can transform your approach to public speaking. It begins with guided imagery—a process where you create a detailed mental picture of your speaking environment. Picture yourself stepping into the room, feeling the ground beneath your feet, and seeing the audience seated before you. Visualize the arrangement of chairs, the lighting, and even the expressions on the faces looking back at you. Imagine the audience engaged and responsive, nodding in agreement and smiling at your anecdotes. This vivid imagery familiarizes your mind with the setting, reducing the element of surprise and making the environment feel more welcoming. The more realistic your mental scene, the more your brain accepts it as reality, significantly easing anxiety.

Visualization isn't just about preparation—it's also rehearsal. Mentally walk through your presentation, from your opening lines to your final call to action. Anticipate potential hurdles, such as unexpected questions or technical difficulties, and imagine handling them with poise and confidence. This practice builds familiarity and reduces anxiety, much like athletes who mentally run through their routines before competitions. By the time you step onto the stage, it will feel like you've already succeeded, making the experience less intimidating and more empowering.

Incorporating affirmations and positive self-talk can bolster the benefits of visualization. Craft affirmations that resonate with your goals, such as "I am a confident and engaging speaker" or "I connect effortlessly with my audience." Repeating these daily helps replace doubt with assurance and sets a constructive tone for your day. Think of affirmations as mental fuel, preparing you for every interaction. The power of these words lies not only in their meaning but in their ability to reshape your internal dialogue, transforming fear into empowerment.

For even greater impact, combine visualization with relaxation techniques. Progressive muscle relaxation, where you tense and release each muscle group from your toes upward, can calm your physical responses. As you do this, visualize yourself speaking confidently, engaging with your audience, and maintaining their interest. Pair this with deep breathing: inhale slowly through your nose, hold for four counts, and exhale through your mouth. This dual approach aligns your mind and body, creating a state of calm, alertness, and readiness.

When practiced consistently, these techniques can transform your perspective on public speaking. Visualization shifts your focus from potential pitfalls to possibilities of success, reframing public speaking as an opportunity to connect and inspire. Over time, what once seemed daunting will become a platform for expression and influence, helping you face your audience with confidence and clarity.

1.5 Power Posing and Physical Readiness

The connection between body and mind plays a pivotal role in public speaking. How you carry yourself physically influences how you feel mentally, and this connection can be leveraged to boost your confidence. One effective method is power posing, popularized by Amy Cuddy's research, which suggests that adopting expansive, open postures can enhance feelings of power. While debates continue about its physiological effects, the psychological benefits remain compelling. When you stand tall, shoulders back, and chin up, your body signals confidence to your brain. This mental shift helps prepare you to face your audience with assurance. Consider using affirmations, visualizing success, and reflecting on your past accomplishments as tools to boost self-assurance.

Incorporating power poses into your preparation routine is both practical and empowering. The "Wonder Woman" pose—standing with feet hip-width apart, hands on hips, and chest lifted—is a classic example. Expansive stretches, such as reaching your arms wide or toward the sky, can also help release tension and create a sense of openness. These poses are more than just physical stances; they're a way to cultivate an empowered mindset. By making them part of your pre-speech ritual, you harness your body's natural capabilities to elevate your mental state.

Physical readiness goes beyond posture—it's about preparing your body to support your speaking performance. Regular exercise boosts energy levels, enhances stamina, and improves overall well-being, all of which contribute to projecting confidence. Maintaining good posture and practicing diaphragmatic breathing are equally vital. A straight spine allows optimal breath support, which is crucial for a clear and powerful voice. Controlled breathing also helps manage nerves, ensuring a steady, composed delivery. Together, these practices reinforce both your physical and mental readiness. Confidence is cultivated not just in practice but also in embracing vulnerability. Techniques like visualization, positive self-talk, and recognizing past wins can help reinforce confidence.

Power poses don't have to be limited to pre-speech moments. Incorporating them into your daily life can build long-term confidence. Practice these poses during your morning routine or before important meetings. Over time, you'll notice changes in how you carry yourself and how others perceive you. This consistent practice cultivates a habit of self-assurance that extends beyond public speaking, positively influencing other areas of your life.

As you integrate these practices, remember that physical readiness is a foundation for effective communication. Preparing your body helps prepare your mind, creating a harmonious balance that enhances your speaking abilities. Each power pose, each controlled breath, and each step forward build your confidence, helping you engage, influence, and lead with authenticity and presence. By embracing the connection between body and mind, you'll find strength in your posture, clarity in your voice, and assurance in your message.

Chapter Two

Crafting Your Unique Voice

I n a busy conference room, a business professional stood before an audience, her voice clear and her message resonant. But this confidence was hard-earned. In her early speaking days, she struggled to find her footing, often mimicking seasoned speakers, believing imitation was the key to success. Over time, however, she discovered her true superpower: authenticity. Her journey underscores an essential truth—your unique voice is your most valuable asset in public speaking. Authenticity not only sets you apart but also fosters genuine connections with your audience. It allows them to see you as a real person with meaningful insights. True confidence is built through both preparation and stepping outside your comfort zone. By integrating these techniques into your routine, you build long-term confidence.

This chapter is about uncovering that voice, embracing it, and letting it become the foundation of your speaking style.

2.1 Discovering Your Authentic Speaking Style

Discovering your authentic speaking style begins with understanding your personal strengths and characteristics. Every speaker has unique qualities that can enhance their communication. Perhaps you have a knack for storytelling, a calm demeanor that puts others at ease, or a dynamic energy that captures attention. These strengths are your tools—the elements that make your voice distinct. Storytelling serves as the bridge between facts and emotions, allowing the audience to visualize and internalize the message. Adding a vivid description or a relatable personal anecdote can make the message even more memorable. Think of a moment when a story changed your perspective—it is this transformation that storytelling brings to public speaking.

Self-assessment is a powerful way to uncover these qualities. Reflect on past speaking experiences and note what felt natural versus what felt forced. What feedback have you received from colleagues, mentors, or friends? Positive comments often highlight your authentic strengths, while constructive criticism can point to areas that may need adjustment. This process of introspection and feedback is the first step toward authenticity.

Challenging self-limiting beliefs is another crucial part of this journey. Negative thoughts, such as "I'll never be good at public speaking," can hold you back. Cognitive Behavioral Therapy (CBT) techniques can help reframe these beliefs into empowering affirmations. For example, replace "I'll never be good" with "I'm improving every time I practice." This shift in perspective fosters growth and keeps you focused on progress.

To reinforce these positive changes, consider keeping a journal. Use it to document your thoughts, track your speaking experiences, and celebrate small victories—whether it's delivering a speech without stumbling or receiving positive feedback. Over time, these moments will build confidence and remind you of your ability to improve and succeed. Confidence is cultivated not just in practice but also in embracing vulnerability. Consider using affirmations, visualizing success, and reflecting on your past accomplishments as tools to boost self-assurance.

Leaning Into Your Personality

Understanding your personality traits can provide further insight into your authentic speaking style. Tools like the **Myers-Briggs Type Indicator** or the **Big Five Personality Traits** can illuminate how you naturally communicate.

- **Introverts** may find strength in thoughtful, deliberate communication, using quiet confidence to engage audiences. Confidence is cultivated not just in practice but also in embracing vulnerability. Consider using affirmations, visualizing success, and reflecting on your past accomplishments as tools to boost self-assurance. By repeating these actions, you reinforce your ability to speak with assurance.

- **Extroverts**, on the other hand, may draw energy from their audience, using charisma and enthusiasm to captivate.

Embrace these traits rather than trying to conform to someone else's style. Tailor your speaking approach to what feels natural for you, as this authenticity will resonate more powerfully with your audience.

The Power of Feedback

Peer feedback is invaluable when honing your authentic voice. Trusted colleagues, mentors, or friends can provide objective insights into your strengths and opportunities for growth. They may notice qualities you overlook or suggest tweaks that elevate your presentation.

Engaging in constructive feedback sessions doesn't mean changing who you are—it's about enhancing how you present yourself. Use this feedback to experiment with different approaches while staying true to your core identity.

Self-Assessment Exercise

Take a moment to reflect on a recent speaking engagement.

- What aspects of your delivery felt natural?

- Which parts seemed forced or out of alignment with your personality?

Write down **three strengths** you believe you possess as a speaker. Then, compare these observations with the feedback you've received from others. Are there recurring themes or patterns in their comments? Use this exercise to align your self-perception with external observations, identifying the areas where your authentic voice shines brightest.

Your unique voice is not just a tool—it's your superpower. Embracing authenticity in public speaking allows you to connect with your audience on a deeper level, transforming each engagement into a meaningful interaction. As you continue to explore and refine your authentic style, you'll find that public speaking becomes less about following a formula and more about expressing who you truly are.

By leveraging your strengths, challenging limiting beliefs, and seeking feedback, you'll craft a speaking style that is not only effective but also uniquely yours. Let authenticity be the foundation upon which you build your confidence and influence. Confidence is cultivated not just in practice but also in embracing vulnerability. Consider using affirmations, visualizing success, and reflecting on your past accomplishments as tools to boost self-assurance.

2.2 Leveraging Personal Stories for Impact

Imagine standing in front of a group, ready to share an experience that changed your life. The room is silent, and all eyes are on you. This is your moment to captivate, to make your story resonate. However, selecting the right personal story is essential. It must be more than meaningful to you—it needs to connect with your audience. The story should speak to their experiences, challenges, or aspirations, aligning with what they value most.

Ask yourself: What does your audience need? Are they seeking inspiration, solutions, or simply a sense of connection? Choose a story that meets those needs, offering insights or encouragement. **Emotional resonance** is just as crucial. A story that evokes feelings—whether joy, empathy, or motivation—leaves a lasting impression. Consider the emotions you want to stir in your listeners and select a narrative that naturally brings those feelings to the surface.

Reframing Personal Narratives

Reframing your experiences through storytelling is a powerful way to engage your audience. Take, for example, a past failure—perhaps you stumbled during an important presentation and left feeling defeated.

Instead of framing it as a setback, turn it into a story of growth: Storytelling serves as the bridge between facts and emotions, allowing the audience to visualize and internalize the message. Adding a vivid description or a relatable personal anecdote can make the message even more memorable. Think of a moment when a story changed your perspective—it is this transformation that storytelling brings to public speaking.

"My first speech was rough, but it taught me the importance of preparation. Now, I thrive in similar situations because of what I learned from that moment."

This reframing achieves two things: it highlights your personal growth and humanizes you, making your story relatable and genuine. Moments of vulnerability, when framed as lessons, become a testament to your resilience and adaptability—qualities that resonate universally.

Structuring Your Story for Maximum Engagement

Once you've selected a story, structuring it effectively ensures it lands with impact. Every great story has a natural flow: a beginning, middle, and end.

1. **Set the Scene**: Start by painting a vivid picture. Use sensory details to describe the sights, sounds, and emotions you experienced. Draw your audience into the world you're describing and help them see it through your eyes.

2. **Build Suspense**: As your story unfolds, create intrigue and anticipation. Keep your listeners curious about what happens next.

3. **Deliver a Meaningful Conclusion**: Tie the ending back to your key message or lesson. Leave your audience with something to think about or act upon.

This structure ensures clarity while maximizing the emotional and intellectual impact of your story.

The Power of Vulnerability in Storytelling:

Storytelling serves as the bridge between facts and emotions, allowing the audience to visualize and internalize the message. Adding a vivid description or a relatable personal anecdote can make the message even more memorable. Think of a moment when a story changed your perspective—it is this transformation that storytelling brings to public speaking.

Vulnerability is one of the most compelling aspects of storytelling. Sharing personal challenges and expressing emotions honestly allows you to forge a deep connection with your audience. Vulnerability demonstrates that you're human—flawed, relatable, and authentic. Storytelling serves as the bridge between facts and emotions, allowing the audience to visualize and internalize the message. Adding a vivid description or a relatable personal anecdote can make the message even more memorable. Think of a moment when a story changed your perspective—it is this transformation that storytelling brings to public speaking.

When you share your struggles, you invite empathy and trust. Your audience sees themselves in your experiences, creating a sense of mutual understanding and support. Vulnerability also encourages others to open up, fostering a shared environment of honesty and growth. These emotionally honest moments are often the most memorable and impactful, lingering in your audience's minds long after the presentation ends.

Balancing Personal and Professional Narratives

While personal stories are powerful, balancing them with professional insights enhances your credibility and impact. Personal anecdotes should seamlessly connect to lessons or principles relevant to your field.

For example, you might share how a childhood love for storytelling inspired your career in communications, where you now use those same skills to engage audiences. By weaving personal and professional elements together, you create a cohesive narrative that is both relatable and informative. Storytelling serves as the bridge between facts and emotions, allowing the audience to visualize and internalize the message. Adding a vivid description or a relatable personal anecdote can make the message even more memorable. Think of a moment when a story changed your perspective—it is this transformation that storytelling brings to public speaking.

Every story you tell should tie back to your central theme or message. This not only reinforces your points but also keeps your presentation focused and meaningful. Balancing personal vulnerability with professional insights enriches your presentation, making it both engaging and enlightening.

Stories are much more than tools for communication—they are bridges between you and your audience. They convey information, foster empathy, and inspire action. Whether you're sharing a personal triumph or a professional insight, your stories have the power to influence and transform.

As you develop your storytelling skills, remember that every story you tell is an opportunity to connect, inspire, and leave a lasting impact. Make your stories count. Storytelling serves as the bridge between facts and emotions, allowing the audience to visualize and internalize the message. Adding a vivid description or a relatable personal anecdote can make the message even more memorable. Think of a moment when a story changed your perspective—storytelling brings this transformation to public speaking.

2.3 Building Emotional Connections with Your Audience

Public speaking is not just about delivering information; it's about forging a connection with your audience on an emotional level. When you tap into their emotions, your message becomes more than words—it becomes an experience. The first step is understanding your audience. Who are they? What are their backgrounds, interests, and needs? Go beyond surface-level demographics to uncover what truly resonates with them. Are they seeking inspiration, reassurance, or motivation to act? Your ability to identify and tap into these emotional triggers can transform a standard presentation into a memorable, impactful experience.

At the heart of this connection lies **empathy**. Putting yourself in your audience's shoes allows you to understand their perspectives and feelings. Active listening plays a key role here, even during your presentation. Observe their verbal and non-verbal cues: Are they nodding, smiling, or furrowing their brows in confusion? These signals are real-time feedback on how your message is landing. Responding to these cues shows you value their input and are willing to adapt. This responsiveness builds trust and rapport, creating a shared experience where your audience feels seen and understood.

Empathy goes beyond observation—it's about genuine emotional engagement. When you connect with your audience's feelings, you create an environment of mutual understanding that leaves a lasting impression.

Incorporating emotions into your storytelling is an art. Use **metaphors and analogies** to make abstract ideas relatable and tangible. For example, compare starting a new project to planting a seed and watching it grow. These universal themes evoke emotions like excitement, fear, or hope that transcend differences and unite your audience. Emotional storytelling creates a bridge between your ideas and your listeners, making your message not only understandable but unforgettable. Storytelling serves as the bridge between facts and emotions, allowing the audience to visualize and internalize the message. Adding a vivid description or a relatable personal anecdote can make the message even more memorable. Think of a moment when a story changed your perspective—it is this transformation that storytelling brings to public speaking.

Audience interaction further deepens this connection. Use open-ended questions to spark curiosity and reflection. For instance, ask your audience to consider how the topic applies to their own lives. Giving them moments to pause and reflect encourages active participation, transforming passive listeners into engaged participants. This involvement fosters a sense of ownership and personal connection to your message.

Emotional connections are the threads that weave your presentation into your audience's lives. They are the moments when your words resonate, your stories inspire, and your message lingers. By practicing empathy, crafting emotional stories, and encouraging interaction, you transform a simple speech into a shared, impactful experience—one that stays with your audience long after the presentation ends.

2.4 Integrating Humor Naturally and Effectively

In public speaking, humor is like a breath of fresh air—it breaks the tension, fosters connection, and transforms your presentation into a memorable experience. Humor is not just about getting a laugh; it's about creating a moment of shared joy that strengthens the bond between you and your audience. Whether it's a chuckle that relaxes the room or a hearty laugh that builds rapport, humor ensures your message sticks in the minds of your listeners. But effective humor isn't about telling jokes—it's about finding a style that feels authentic to you and aligns with your message.

Observational humor is one of the most relatable forms, drawing from the quirks of everyday life. Pointing out the universal struggles of Mondays or the peculiarities of corporate jargon can resonate with nearly any audience. These shared experiences create a sense of camaraderie. **Self-deprecating humor** is another approach where you gently poke fun at yourself. It shows humility and self-awareness, endearing you to your audience. However, balance is key—keep it lighthearted and avoid diminishing your credibility. The goal is to connect, not to undermine yourself.

Balancing humor with your message requires finesse. Think of humor as a spice—too much can overwhelm you, while too little leaves your presentation bland. Introduce humor at natural breaks in your narrative, such as transitioning between topics or lightening a complex idea. For example, a humorous anecdote about a past mistake can make a heavy subject more approachable. Context is everything—what works for one audience may fall flat with another. Understanding your audience's preferences, sensitivities, and cultural context ensures your humor lands effectively.

Practicing humor delivery is as critical as crafting the humor itself. Timing is essential—a well-placed pause after a humorous remark allows the laughter to resonate, while rushing can dilute the impact. Rehearse with diverse audiences to see what elicits laughter and what doesn't. Solicit feedback on your humor's effectiveness, and use these insights to refine your delivery. Practice helps ensure that your humor feels natural, not forced.

When humor aligns with your authentic voice, it elevates your presentation. It humanizes you, making your message more relatable and memorable. Shared laughter fosters a sense of connection and joy, leaving your audience with not just your message but a positive emotional experience. When used effectively, humor transforms your presentation from informative to unforgettable.

2.5 Maintaining Authenticity Across Different Settings

Navigating diverse environments while staying true to yourself is a crucial skill for any speaker. Each setting presents unique dynamics, and understanding these nuances is key to adapting effectively. Start by analyzing your audience and the context of your presentation. Are you addressing a small team meeting or delivering a keynote at a large conference? Each scenario requires a tailored approach. Consider the audience's expectations, cultural background, and the formality of the event. This analysis helps you adjust your language, tone, and delivery to resonate deeply without compromising your authenticity.

Adapting doesn't mean changing who you are—it means refining your style to meet your audience's needs while staying true to your core message. It's about finding the balance between honoring the setting and retaining the unique qualities that make your voice stand out.

Consistency in Personal Branding

In today's interconnected world, consistency in your personal brand is essential for maintaining authenticity across platforms. Your online presence should align with your in-person communication, creating a cohesive and trustworthy image. Whether you're posting on social media, networking at an event, or speaking on stage, your core values and voice should remain consistent.

Think of your personal brand as a narrative that ties together all aspects of your communication. By aligning your digital and physical personas, you build a reliable identity that your audience can trust. For example, if your public speaking emphasizes inclusivity and collaboration, ensure that these values are reflected in your online posts and interactions. This alignment creates a unified and authentic persona, strengthening your connection with audiences across all touchpoints.

Cultural Sensitivity and Authenticity Adopting a mindset of global awareness enriches communication. Being open to learning about traditions, social cues, and language nuances allows for deeper connections. Engaging with diverse groups gives you insights that shape your message to resonate universally.

Engaging with culturally diverse audiences requires a thoughtful approach that balances authenticity with sensitivity. Research is your greatest ally here. Understanding cultural norms, customs, and communication preferences allows you to connect respectfully and meaningfully.

For instance, some cultures value direct communication, while others prefer a more indirect or formal approach. Tailoring your style to align with these preferences demonstrates respect and thoughtfulness. However, maintaining authenticity doesn't mean losing your unique voice—it means finding a way to honor cultural differences while staying true to your identity.

The key is to embrace diversity and use it to enrich your message. Integrating cultural awareness into your communication fosters deeper connections and ensures your message resonates with varied audiences.

Flexibility Without Compromising Authenticity

Flexibility is a hallmark of authentic communication. Adapting to different settings doesn't require you to lose your core identity; instead, it enables you to connect effectively with a variety of audiences.

Some settings may call for a more formal tone, while others might benefit from a conversational approach. For example, when presenting at a corporate meeting, you might opt for polished language and structured delivery. Conversely, speaking at a community event might call for warmth and relatability. While the tone and format may shift, your core message and personal style remain intact.

Preserve key elements of your authenticity—your tone, storytelling approach, or sense of humor—while making necessary adjustments. This adaptability ensures that you remain relatable and engaging, no matter the environment. Storytelling serves as the bridge between facts and emotions, allowing the audience to visualize and internalize the message. Adding a vivid description or a relatable personal anecdote can make the message even more memorable. Think of a moment when a story changed your perspective—it is this transformation that storytelling brings to public speaking.

Authenticity is your anchor in any speaking situation. It's what makes your communication genuine, effective, and memorable. By understanding your audience, maintaining a consistent personal brand, respecting cultural differences, and embracing flexibility, you can connect with any audience without compromising who you are.

Your ability to maintain authenticity across diverse settings not only enhances your public speaking but also strengthens your overall communication skills. It enables you to navigate varied contexts with confidence, leaving a lasting impression wherever you go. Confidence is cultivated not just through practice but also through embracing vulnerability. Consider using affirmations, visualizing success, and reflecting on your past accomplishments as tools to boost self-assurance.

In the next chapter, we'll delve into the art of storytelling—a powerful tool for captivating and influencing audiences and an essential element of your public speaking arsenal. Storytelling serves as the bridge between facts and emotions, allowing the audience to visualize and internalize the message. Adding a vivid description or a relatable personal anecdote can make the message even more memorable. Think of a moment when a story changed your perspective—it is this transformation that storytelling brings to public speaking.

Chapter Three

Mastering Storytelling

Imagine you're at a networking event surrounded by industry leaders and potential clients. The air hums with conversation, a symphony of voices, each vying for attention. Amidst this, one individual steps forward, sharing a story that captures the room. The story is not just a recount of events but a narrative that resonates, leaving a lasting impression. This is the power of storytelling. It transcends the mere transfer of information, creating connections and sparking inspiration. In this chapter, we dive into the art of choosing the right story, a vital skill for any professional looking to enhance their communication and influence.

3.1 The Art of Story Selection: Finding the Right Narrative

Imagine you're at a networking event surrounded by industry leaders and potential clients. The air buzzes with conversation—a symphony of voices vying for attention. Amidst this, someone steps forward and shares a story. But it's not just any story—it's a narrative that resonates, capturing the room and leaving a lasting impression. This is the power of storytelling: it transforms information into connection, inspiration, and influence. Storytelling serves as the bridge between facts and emotions, allowing the audience to visualize and internalize the message. Adding a vivid description or a relatable personal anecdote can make the message even more memorable. Think of a moment when a story changed your perspective—it is this transformation that storytelling brings to public speaking.

The foundation of great storytelling lies in choosing the right story. This begins with defining your **purpose**. What message do you want to convey? Is it a lesson in perseverance, a call for innovation, or a celebration of collaboration? Your story should align seamlessly with your objectives, serving as the backbone of your presentation. A purposeful narrative provides context and depth, turning abstract ideas into tangible insights. By selecting stories that reinforce your message, you ensure your narrative is not only engaging but also impactful. Storytelling serves as the bridge between facts and emotions, allowing the audience to visualize and internalize the message. Adding a vivid description or a relatable personal anecdote can make the message even more memorable. Think of a moment when a story changed your perspective—it is this transformation that storytelling brings to public speaking.

Understanding Your Audience

Knowing your audience is essential to selecting a story that resonates. Start by conducting a thorough demographic analysis. Are you speaking to seasoned professionals, fresh graduates, or a mix of both? Each group brings distinct perspectives and expectations. Tailor your story to their experiences, aspirations, and challenges.

Dig deeper into their values and needs. What matters most to them? What problems are they trying to solve? When your story aligns with these insights, it feels personal and relevant, fostering engagement. When your audience sees themselves reflected in your story, they're more likely to connect with your message and take it to heart. This shared experience transforms passive listeners into active participants, creating a powerful bond that strengthens your narrative.

Balancing Novelty and Familiarity

Striking the right balance between novelty and familiarity is a delicate art in storytelling. A unique anecdote grabs attention and offers fresh perspectives or unexpected insights. However, it's equally important to ground your story in universal themes that your audience can relate to. Storytelling serves as the bridge between facts and emotions, allowing the audience to visualize and internalize the message. Adding a vivid description or a relatable personal anecdote can make the message even more memorable. Think of a moment when a story changed your perspective—it is this transformation that storytelling brings to public speaking.

Avoid falling into the trap of clichés, as they can dilute your message and disengage your listeners. Instead, aim for stories that surprise while maintaining a thread of familiarity. For instance, you might weave a personal anecdote about an unexpected challenge into a larger theme of resilience or teamwork—ideas your audience can easily connect with. By blending originality with relatability, you create a storytelling tapestry that captivates and resonates, leaving a memorable impression. Storytelling serves as the bridge between facts and emotions, allowing the audience to visualize and internalize the message. Adding a vivid description or a relatable personal anecdote can make the message even more memorable. Think of a moment when a story changed your perspective—it is this transformation that storytelling brings to public speaking.

Evaluating Impact: Emotional and Logical Appeal

The most effective stories engage both the heart and the mind. Evaluate your story's potential by considering its emotional and logical appeal.

- **Emotional Appeal**: Does your story evoke feelings of empathy, excitement, or curiosity? Emotional triggers draw your audience in and help them connect with the narrative on a deeper level.

- **Logical Appeal**: Does your story have a clear structure that guides your audience through its message? A logical flow ensures clarity, helping your audience follow along without confusion.

A powerful story combines these elements, presenting complex ideas in a way that is both engaging and easy to understand. This combination not only captivates but also persuades, amplifying your ability to influence and inspire.

Story Selection Checklist

Before finalizing your story, ask yourself the following:

- **Purpose Alignment**: Does the story align with your key message and objectives?

- **Audience Relevance**: Is it tailored to the demographics, interests, and challenges of your audience?

- **Novelty and Familiarity**: Does it offer a unique perspective while remaining relatable?

- **Emotional and Logical Appeal**: Does it engage emotions and provide clarity through a structured flow?

Incorporating these elements into your storytelling approach ensures your narrative not only engages but also influences, inspiring your audience to think, feel, and act. Mastering the art of story selection is a powerful tool in your public speaking repertoire, one that can elevate your communication and amplify your impact.

3.2 Structuring Your Story: The Perfect Arc

Crafting a story that captivates and holds your audience's attention requires mastering the narrative arc. This arc, much like the graceful flight of a bird, guides your story from an engaging introduction through rising conflict to a satisfying resolution. At the outset, you set the stage, introducing characters and context. Here, you plant seeds of curiosity, inviting your audience to follow along. As the story unfolds, tension builds—like a symphony swelling to its crescendo—drawing your listeners deeper into the narrative. Finally, the resolution ties everything together, offering closure and insight. This journey mirrors the human experience, making your story both relatable and unforgettable.

A compelling story begins with a powerful **introduction**. The opening moments are where you hook your audience and draw them into your world. Start with a bold statement, a surprising fact, or a thought-provoking question. Alternatively, use vivid descriptions to immerse your listeners in the scene. For example, describe the setting, the mood, and the characters with sensory-rich details. This approach not only grabs attention but also creates a foundation for a story that resonates. An engaging beginning ensures your audience is eager to hear more.

The **climax** is the heartbeat of your story, where tension peaks and emotions run high. Building to this moment requires careful pacing, like a conductor guiding an orchestra through a dramatic score. Introduce key revelations at moments of maximum impact, keeping your audience on edge as the narrative unfolds. Use pacing techniques to heighten suspense, drawing out moments of tension and releasing them with precision. The climax is more than a high point—it's the emotional core of your story, leaving a lasting impression on your audience.

A well-crafted **conclusion** provides more than closure—it reinforces your message and leaves your audience with something meaningful to ponder. Tie your ending back to your opening hook, creating a full-circle moment that underscores your core idea. Offer a clear takeaway or call to action, ensuring your story has a purpose beyond entertainment. This thoughtful conclusion helps your audience internalize your message, making it relevant to their own lives.

When each element—introduction, climax, and resolution—is carefully crafted, your story transcends mere words. It becomes an experience, one that captivates, inspires, and leaves a lasting impact.

3.3 Emotional Triggers: Crafting Stories that Resonate

Public speaking is more than conveying information—it's about evoking emotions that deeply resonate with your audience. **Emotional triggers** such as hope, fear, and empathy tap into universal human experiences, making your message relatable and memorable.

- **Hope** inspires and motivates your audience, encouraging them to envision a brighter future or a shared goal.

- **Fear** highlights challenges and risks, urging them to take action or consider alternative paths.

- **Empathy** bridges the divide, fostering understanding and connection by making your audience feel seen and heard.

Aligning these emotional triggers with your message ensures that your story not only informs but also influences. This alignment transforms your narrative into a powerful tool for inspiration and action.

To make your stories vivid and immersive, incorporate **sensory details** that bring your narrative to life. Use language that engages the imagination:

- Describe visuals, like the golden glow of a sunrise or the sharp angles of a skyscraper.

- Evoke sounds, such as the gentle rustling of leaves or the hum of distant city traffic.

- Appeal to touch with sensations like the smoothness of polished marble or the roughness of a cobblestone street.

- Engage the sense of smell or taste with imagery, such as the aroma of freshly brewed coffee or the tang of salty sea air.

Metaphors and similes can further enhance this imagery. For example, compare a busy office to a beehive or a moment of calm to a still lake. These details, inspired by techniques like Cognitive Behavioral Therapy (CBT), evoke emotions and make your story feel alive and tangible.

Balancing emotion and logic is essential for effective storytelling. Emotions captivate the heart, while logic persuades the mind. Blending these elements creates a narrative that resonates on multiple levels. Use anecdotes to humanize data, transforming abstract statistics into relatable stories. Share personal experiences or client journeys to illustrate points, making your message grounded and real. This combination of emotional and logical appeal ensures your story is both compelling and convincing, encouraging deep engagement with your ideas. Storytelling serves as the bridge between facts and emotions, allowing the audience to visualize and internalize the message. Adding a vivid description or a relatable personal anecdote can make the message even more memorable. Think of a moment when a story changed your perspective—it is this transformation that storytelling brings to public speaking.

While emotions are powerful tools, they must be used **ethically**. Avoid manipulation, which undermines trust and credibility. Authenticity is the foundation of ethical storytelling. Share narratives that reflect your true experiences and beliefs, respecting your audience's intelligence and autonomy. Trust your listeners to connect with your story naturally without forcing a specific reaction. This respect fosters a relationship built on trust, enhancing your influence and impact. Storytelling serves as the bridge between facts and emotions, allowing the audience to visualize and internalize the message. Adding a vivid description or a relatable personal anecdote can make the message even more memorable. Think of a moment when a story changed your perspective—it is this transformation that storytelling brings to public speaking.

By tapping into emotional triggers, balancing them with logic, and maintaining authenticity, you create stories that resonate deeply. These narratives don't just inform—they inspire, influence, and leave a lasting impression.

3.4 Storytelling for Technical Presentations

Storytelling serves as the bridge between facts and emotions, allowing the audience to visualize and internalize the message. Adding a vivid description or a relatable personal anecdote can make the message even more memorable. Think of a moment when a story changed your perspective—it is this transformation that storytelling brings to public speaking.

Technical presentations often face a unique challenge: presenting complex information in a way that is accessible and engaging. You may have detailed data, intricate processes, and comprehensive analyses to share, but your audience might lack the technical expertise to fully grasp the material. How can you ensure your message is both clear and compelling?

One powerful technique is using **analogies and metaphors**. These tools bridge the gap between the complex and the familiar, making intricate ideas easier to understand. For example, explaining a neural network in artificial intelligence can be likened to a human brain learning through experience. This comparison anchors abstract concepts in relatable imagery, enabling your audience to connect with the subject matter on a deeper level. Analogies and metaphors provide clarity, transforming technical jargon into ideas that resonate.

Structuring Technical Content as a Narrative

Breaking down technical information into a **step-by-step story** creates a logical flow that keeps your audience engaged. Instead of overwhelming listeners with raw data, guide them on a journey—from identifying a problem to reaching a solution. Highlight key milestones along the way, illustrating each phase of your explanation with clear, sequential steps.

Think of your presentation as a narrative, where each piece builds upon the last. This approach not only organizes information effectively but also makes it easier to digest. For instance, a presentation on the implementation of a new software system could start with the challenge it addresses, move through the development and deployment phases, and conclude with measurable results. Each step acts as a building block, constructing a complete picture in your audience's mind.

By framing technical content as a story, you transform dense material into a narrative that informs and captivates simultaneously.

Emphasizing Human Impact

One of the most compelling ways to enhance a technical presentation is by emphasizing its **human impact**. Audiences connect more deeply with stories that affect real people. Share examples of how your technical work has influenced stakeholders or improved lives.

For instance, discuss how a software application increased team productivity or how a technology reduced environmental impact.

These personal accounts provide context and authenticity, illustrating the tangible benefits of your work. They transform abstract data into relatable outcomes, fostering empathy and engagement. By putting a face to the numbers, you make your presentation more meaningful and memorable. Emerging technologies like virtual and augmented reality are also reshaping how audiences interact with presentations. By experimenting with these tools, speakers can create immersive experiences that go beyond traditional slides and visuals. Such innovations can leave a lasting impact when used thoughtfully.

Balancing Detail and Narrative Flow

It is essential to maintain narrative flow while balancing technical detail. Prioritize key information that supports your core message, resisting the temptation to include every minute detail. Determine which points are crucial for understanding and which can be simplified or omitted.

Visual aids play a vital role here. Use diagrams, charts, and images to illustrate complex concepts succinctly. These visuals complement your storytelling, providing visual cues that aid comprehension without overshadowing your narrative. A well-chosen graphic can explain in seconds what might take minutes to describe verbally. Storytelling serves as the bridge between facts and emotions, allowing the audience to visualize and internalize the message. Adding a vivid description or a relatable personal anecdote can make the message even more memorable. Think of a moment when a story changed your perspective—it is this transformation that storytelling brings to public speaking.

By strategically selecting details and leveraging visuals, you create a streamlined narrative that communicates effectively without overwhelming your audience.

Adapting for Non-Technical Audiences

Engaging non-technical audiences requires tailoring your language and examples to match their knowledge level. Avoid jargon or overly technical terms that could alienate listeners. Instead, use **clear, simple language** that conveys your message without sacrificing accuracy.

Relatable comparisons and anecdotes further bridge the gap between technical content and everyday understanding. For example, describe data encryption as a "digital lock and key" to explain cybersecurity concepts. These familiar elements make your presentation accessible and inclusive, ensuring every audience member feels informed and valued.

By adapting your approach to meet diverse audience needs, you enhance engagement and ensure your message is understood by all.

Through these techniques, technical presentations can transform from data-heavy lectures into engaging stories that resonate. By combining analogies, structured narratives, human impact, and tailored language, you create presentations that not only inform but also inspire. With these strategies, even the most complex topics can captivate and connect with your audience.

3.5 Using Data to Tell Compelling Stories

In today's data-driven world, numbers and statistics can illuminate insights or obscure meaning. The key is to transform raw data into narratives that captivate and inform. Instead of overwhelming your audience with spreadsheets or dense charts, look for the stories hidden within the numbers.

Trends often serve as the foundation of these stories. Whether it's a pattern of growth, a sudden decline, or seasonal fluctuations, trends reveal narratives that highlight key insights. For example, an upward trend in customer satisfaction scores over time could tell a story of improved service strategies. By identifying and emphasizing these trends, you can create narratives that resonate with your audience. Relate these stories to real-world applications—how the data impacts decisions, drives strategies, or shapes outcomes. When data is connected to practical, tangible results, it transitions from abstract figures to meaningful insights that engage your listeners.

The Art of Visual Storytelling with Data:

Storytelling serves as the bridge between facts and emotions, allowing the audience to visualize and internalize the message. Adding a vivid description or a relatable personal anecdote can make the message even more memorable. Think of a moment when a story changed your perspective—it is this transformation that storytelling brings to public speaking.

Visual storytelling is a powerful way to make complex data accessible and engaging. **Charts** and **infographics** distill intricate information into visuals that are easy to digest and retain. A well-designed chart doesn't just present data—it guides your audience's understanding by highlighting key points and trends. Storytelling serves as the bridge between facts and emotions, allowing the audience to visualize and internalize the message. Adding a vivid description or a relatable personal anecdote can make the message even more memorable. Think of a moment when a story changed your perspective—it is this transformation that storytelling brings to public speaking.

Infographics go one step further, blending visuals with text to tell a story at a glance. For instance, an infographic showing the reduction in energy consumption over a year can quickly communicate progress and impact. Visualizing data changes over time—whether it's illustrating progress, highlighting challenges, or showcasing achievements—helps your audience grasp the bigger picture.

By combining clarity with creativity, visual storytelling enhances your ability to captivate and inform. It ensures your audience not only understands the data but also remembers the key takeaways. Storytelling serves as the bridge between facts and emotions, allowing the audience to visualize and internalize the message. Adding a vivid description or a relatable personal anecdote can make the message even more memorable. Think of a moment when a story changed your perspective—it is this transformation that storytelling brings to public speaking.

Humanizing Data for Deeper Connections

Numbers gain meaning when tied to personal stories, making the abstract tangible. **Case studies** are an excellent way to humanize data by showing how it translates into real-world scenarios. For example, a case study on how data-driven decisions improved a company's productivity creates a relatable narrative for your audience.

Personal testimonials further add an emotional layer to data storytelling. Pairing data with real-life examples—such as how a community benefitted from a policy shift or how an individual's life improved due to technological advancements—creates a stronger connection. These human elements transform data from cold numbers into compelling stories of change, progress, or innovation. When your audience sees how the numbers affect people, they engage with the message on a deeper level. Storytelling serves as the bridge between facts and emotions, allowing the audience to visualize and internalize the message. Adding a vivid description or a relatable personal anecdote can make the message even more memorable. Think of a moment when a story changed your perspective—it is this transformation that storytelling brings to public speaking.

Balancing Accuracy and Narrative

While storytelling enhances the impact of data, maintaining **accuracy and integrity** is paramount. Ethical data storytelling involves presenting information honestly and transparently. Avoid distorting facts to fit a narrative or cherry-picking data to support a biased perspective. Storytelling serves as the bridge between facts and emotions, allowing the audience to visualize and internalize the message. Adding a vivid description or a relatable personal anecdote can make the message even more memorable. Think of a moment when a story changed your perspective—it is this transformation that storytelling brings to public speaking.

Always verify your data sources to ensure they are reliable and unbiased. Fact-checking is essential to building trust with your audience and reinforcing the credibility of your message. A compelling story backed by accurate, well-sourced data has the power to inform and persuade, making your narrative not just engaging but also trustworthy.

When used effectively, data transforms from mere numbers into powerful stories that inform, engage, and inspire. By identifying trends, incorporating visual aids, humanizing statistics, and upholding accuracy, you can create presentations that resonate deeply with your audience.

As you reflect on your own presentations, consider how the stories hidden in your data can drive change, influence decisions, and connect with others on a meaningful level. This chapter has provided you with the tools to turn data into narratives that captivate and inform. Next, we'll explore how to engage your audience and command their attention, building on the storytelling skills you've developed here. Storytelling serves as the bridge between facts and emotions, allowing the audience to visualize and internalize the message. Adding a vivid description or a relatable personal anecdote can make the message even more memorable. Think of a moment when a story changed your perspective—it is this transformation that storytelling brings to public speaking.

Chapter Four

Audience Engagement

As you step onto the stage, the anticipation in the room is palpable. Every eye is on you, waiting to hear what you have to say. This is your moment—not just to deliver a speech, but to truly engage. **Audience engagement** is the heartbeat of any successful presentation. It's the difference between a message that resonates and one that falls flat.

To captivate your audience, you must first understand them. Just as a seasoned chef tailors their dish to the tastes of their guests, you must customize your message to meet the needs and expectations of your listeners. This chapter explores the art of audience understanding and provides actionable strategies to craft messages that connect and captivate.

4.1 Understanding Your Audience: Tailoring Messages

The first step in tailoring your message is conducting thorough **audience research**. Gathering insights about your audience ensures your content speaks directly to them.

Surveys and pre-event questionnaires are powerful tools for this purpose. They can reveal your audience's demographics, interests, and expectations. For example, if you're presenting to tech professionals, understanding their areas of expertise allows you to customize your message to their level of familiarity.

Social media platforms like LinkedIn and Twitter offer another rich source of information. Explore what your audience is discussing—their concerns, challenges, and trending topics in their industry. Addressing these issues in your presentation ensures your content is timely, relevant, and engaging.

Identifying Audience Needs and Interests

Understanding your audience's needs and interests is key to crafting a message that resonates.

1. **Analyze feedback from previous events.**

2. Look for recurring themes in attendees' comments. What did they appreciate, and what did they find lacking? These insights help refine your content to better meet the expectations of your current audience.

3. **Stay informed about industry trends.**

4. Following the latest developments in your field allows you to align your message with what your audience values most. Being knowledgeable and up-to-date not only captures at-

tention but also earns respect.

By tailoring your message to these interests and needs, you position yourself as a relevant and engaging speaker.

4.2 Customizing Content for Different Demographics

Adapting your content to suit different demographics is both an art and a skill.

- **Use relatable examples and anecdotes**: Share stories or case studies that reflect your audience's world. For instance, if you're speaking to educators, examples from classroom experiences will resonate more than corporate anecdotes.

- **Adjust your language and level of technicality**: For a general audience, avoid jargon and use clear, simple explanations. Conversely, a specialized audience may appreciate technical details and industry-specific terminology.

This sensitivity to your audience's background ensures your message is accessible, engaging, and impactful.

- Aligning Your Message with Audience Goals

To truly connect, your presentation objectives must align with your audience's goals.

- **Identify their motivations**: Are they seeking practical solutions, inspiration, or a fresh perspective?

- **Highlight mutual benefits**: Shape your message to demonstrate how it helps your audience achieve their objectives.

When your goals and theirs are aligned, it fosters a sense of partnership. Your audience views your presentation as a valuable tool to help them succeed, building trust and capturing interest.

Audience Research Checklist

To ensure your message resonates, ask yourself the following:

- **Surveys and Questionnaires**: Have you gathered data on your audience's demographics and interests?

- **Social Media Insights**: Are you aware of trending topics and discussions in your audience's industry?

- **Feedback Analysis**: Have you reviewed feedback from previous events to identify common themes?

- **Industry Trends**: Are you informed about the latest developments in your field?

- **Custom Examples**: Are your examples and anecdotes relevant to your audience's experiences?

- **Language Adjustment**: Have you tailored your language and level of technicality to suit your audience?

- **Objective Alignment**: Are your presentation objectives aligned with your audience's goals?

The ability to tailor your message to your audience is what transforms a presentation from a mere speech into a memorable experience. By understanding your audience, identifying their needs, and aligning your message with their goals, you ensure that your content resonates deeply and leaves a lasting impact.

This chapter equips you with the tools to engage your audience on a personal level. In the next section, we'll delve into practical techniques for maintaining attention throughout your presentation, ensuring your audience stays hooked from beginning to end.

4.3 Interactive Techniques to Spark Engagement

Imagine standing before your audience, not as a lecturer but as a conductor orchestrating a symphony of voices and ideas. Audience participation transforms a presentation from a static monologue into a vibrant dialogue. Engaging your audience through interactive techniques creates a dynamic atmosphere where ideas flow freely and every participant feels valued.

Live Polls and Surveys: Fostering Real-Time Involvement

Incorporate real-time polls and surveys to invite your audience to share their thoughts. For instance, you can ask attendees to vote on a topic or rate their interest in a subject. Tools like these foster inclusion and involvement. They not only make your presentation interactive but also provide you with valuable insights into your audience's preferences and concerns.

Imagine starting your talk by asking, "What's the biggest challenge you face in [your field]?" and displaying a live word cloud of their answers. This interaction creates a lively atmosphere and makes your audience feel heard. The feedback you receive can also guide your discussion, ensuring your content aligns with their interests.

Real-Time Q&A: Encouraging Open Dialogue:

A **real-time Q&A session** turns the spotlight on your audience, creating an environment of mutual exchange. Encourage listeners to ask questions and share opinions by fostering a welcoming atmosphere where no query is too basic or complex. Acknowledge each question thoughtfully, using it as a springboard to explore your content further.

For example, if someone asks, "How does this apply to small businesses?" you can expand on the topic with tailored insights. This approach not only clarifies your message but also reinforces your expertise and openness. Q&A sessions build rapport and trust, transforming your presentation into a collaborative exploration of ideas and showing your audience that you value their input.

Interactive Storytelling: Drawing Your Audience In

Storytelling serves as the bridge between facts and emotions, allowing the audience to visualize and internalize the message. Adding a vivid description or a relatable personal anecdote can make the message even more memorable. Think of a moment when a story changed your perspective—it is this transformation that storytelling brings to public speaking.

Storytelling becomes even more powerful when combined with interactive elements. Engage your audience by inviting them to participate in the narrative. For example, pause mid-story to ask, "What would you do in this situation?" or "Has anyone experienced something similar?" These prompts turn your audience into active participants, drawing them deeper into your story. Storytelling serves as the bridge between facts and emotions, allowing the audience to visualize and internalize the message. Adding a vivid description or a relatable personal anecdote can make the message even more memorable. Think of a moment when a story changed your perspective—it is this transformation that storytelling brings to public speaking.

Take it a step further with **story-based problem-solving exercises**. Present a scenario tied to your narrative and challenge your audience to work through it, either individually or in groups. These activities encourage critical thinking and collaboration while reinforcing the story's lessons. By weaving interaction into storytelling, you create an immersive experience that captivates and engages. Storytelling serves as the bridge between facts and emotions, allowing the audience to visualize and internalize the message. Adding a vivid description or a relatable personal anecdote can make the message even more memorable. Think of a moment when a story changed your perspective—it is this transformation that storytelling brings to public speaking.

Group Activities: Encouraging Collaboration

Facilitating **group activities** enhances engagement by allowing participants to interact with the material and each other. Breakout discussions are particularly effective for exploring specific topics, sharing perspectives, and generating new ideas in smaller, more intimate settings.

For example, ask groups to brainstorm solutions to a challenge relevant to your topic and then present their ideas to the room. Hands-on workshops and simulations go even further, enabling participants to apply concepts in real-world scenarios. These formats empower your audience to take charge of their learning, creating a sense of ownership and collaboration.

By designing activities that encourage group participation, you foster a dynamic environment in which every voice is heard and diverse viewpoints are celebrated.

4.4 Leveraging Technology: Enhancing Interaction

Emerging technologies like virtual and augmented reality are also reshaping how audiences interact with presentations. By experimenting with these tools, speakers can create immersive experiences that go beyond traditional slides and visuals. When used thoughtfully, such innovations can leave a lasting impact.

In today's digital age, technology provides innovative ways to enhance audience interaction. **Audience response apps** enable real-time feedback through features like live polling, quizzes, and word clouds. These tools offer multiple ways to engage your audience and adapt your presentation based on their reactions. Emerging technologies like virtual and augmented reality are also reshaping how audiences interact with presentations. By experimenting with these tools, speakers can create immersive experiences that go beyond traditional slides and visuals. Such innovations can leave a lasting impact when used thoughtfully.

For a more immersive experience, consider **virtual reality (VR)** elements. A VR simulation, such as a virtual tour or an interactive demonstration, captivates attention and stimulates curiosity by placing your audience directly in the heart of the action. By integrating technology, you elevate the interactive experience, leaving a lasting impression. Emerging technologies like virtual and augmented reality are also reshaping how audiences interact with presentations. By experimenting with these tools, speakers can create immersive experiences that go beyond traditional slides and visuals. Such innovations can leave a lasting impact when used thoughtfully.

Audience engagement is about more than keeping attention—it's about creating an interactive and collaborative experience that resonates deeply. By incorporating live polls, storytelling, group activities, and cutting-edge technology, you transform your presentation into a memorable dialogue. These techniques empower your audience, making them active participants in the journey and ensuring your message leaves a lasting impact. Storytelling serves as the bridge between facts and emotions, allowing the audience to visualize and internalize the message. Adding a vivid description or a relatable personal anecdote can make the message even more memorable. Think of a moment when a story changed your perspective—it is this transformation that storytelling brings to public speaking. Emerging technologies like virtual and augmented reality are also reshaping how audiences interact with presentations. By experimenting with these tools, speakers can create immersive experiences that go beyond traditional slides and visuals. Such innovations can leave a lasting impact when used thoughtfully.

4.5 The Strategic Use of Pauses and Silence

Silence, often underestimated, holds profound power in public speaking. It's not just the words that matter, but the spaces between them. Strategic pauses can elevate a presentation, enhancing engagement, comprehension, and emotional impact. When you pause, you give your audience a moment to reflect, allowing your message to resonate. In these moments of quiet, your listeners connect the dots, drawing meaning from your words.

A pause can also build suspense, creating anticipation for what's to come. This anticipation keeps your audience on the edge of their seats, eager to hear your next point. By learning to use silence effectively, you can transform your speaking from good to unforgettable.

Timing Your Pauses for Maximum Impact

The timing of your pauses determines their effectiveness. After delivering a significant point, a pause lets the weight of your words settle. This moment of silence emphasizes the importance of your statement, giving your audience time to absorb its relevance.

Pauses also serve as markers for transitions, signaling a shift in topic or perspective. For example, a brief pause before introducing a new idea helps your audience follow the narrative seamlessly. This clarity in structure keeps your listeners engaged and ensures they understand the progression of your presentation.

Mastering the timing of pauses requires both practice and intuition. It involves reading the room—observing your audience's reactions—and adapting your delivery to suit their needs. By timing your pauses effectively, you not only enhance your message but also create a rhythm that captivates and holds attention.

Controlling Pace with Pauses

Pauses play a critical role in managing the pace of your delivery. Slowing down when presenting complex information allows your audience to process intricate details without feeling overwhelmed.

Deliberate pacing ensures clarity, making your message accessible regardless of its complexity. A well-placed pause can also create a conversational tone, inviting your audience to engage in a dialogue rather than passively listening to a monologue. This conversational rhythm fosters a sense of connection, making your audience feel involved and valued.

By using pauses to control the flow of your presentation, you can create a dynamic and engaging experience that will resonate with your listeners.

Practicing the Art of Pauses

Incorporating pauses into your practice sessions is essential for building confidence and proficiency. Start by recording your presentations and paying close attention to the natural rhythm of your speech. Identify where pauses occur organically and consider where additional pauses could enhance your delivery. Confidence is cultivated not just in practice but also in embracing vulnerability. Consider using affirmations, visualizing success, and reflecting on your past accomplishments as tools to boost self-assurance.

Listen to these recordings with a critical ear, focusing on the flow and impact of your speech. This self-assessment helps you pinpoint opportunities to refine your technique. Additionally, seek feedback from trusted colleagues or mentors who can provide insights on how your pauses affect engagement and comprehension.

With consistent practice and constructive feedback, pauses become an integral part of your delivery. Over time, they will enhance your message and strengthen your connection with your audience.

Silence is not an absence of sound but a powerful tool for amplifying meaning. Strategic pauses provide moments for reflection, highlight transitions, and help manage pacing, all while fostering connection and engagement. When used effectively, pauses turn your presentation into a dynamic, memorable experience that resonates long after the final word.

Pause Practice Exercise

1. **Record Your Presentation**: Start by recording a short segment of your presentation. Play it back and identify key moments where a pause could enhance the impact of your delivery.

2. **Experiment with Pauses**: Practice inserting pauses at these moments, varying their length and placement. Observe how these adjustments influence the overall rhythm and engagement of your speech.

3. **Refine Your Timing**: Pay attention to how the pauses allow your audience to reflect or anticipate your next point. Adjust your timing to create a natural, compelling flow.

This exercise develops your intuitive sense of timing, helping you use pauses strategically to enhance your delivery. Pauses are not just empty spaces—they are opportunities to enrich engagement, deepen understanding, and leave a lasting impression.

4.6 Handling Disruptive Audience Members with Grace

Disruptions during a presentation are inevitable, but how you handle them defines your ability to stay composed and maintain control. Anticipating and managing these moments with grace transforms potential challenges into opportunities to connect with your audience.

Identifying Potential Disruptions

Understanding how to spot disruptions before they escalate is key. Look for signs such as:

- Side conversations or distracted body language.

- Audience members focus on their phones instead of you.

Disruptions can stem from confusion over complex topics or a lack of relevance. Anticipating these moments helps you tailor your approach to keep your audience engaged and minimize interruptions.

Responding with Poise

When disruptions occur, respond calmly and confidently. Here's how:

- **Acknowledge and Redirect**: If someone interjects with an unrelated question, respond respectfully while maintaining focus. For instance: *"That's an interesting point, and I'll touch on it shortly, but first, let's finish this section."* This approach validates the individual while keeping the presentation on track.

- **Encourage Questions at Key Moments**: Designate specific times for audience interaction, such as after key points or during a Q&A session. This minimizes interruptions while fostering engagement.

Balancing listening with leadership ensures that questions enrich your presentation rather than derail it.

Staying Composed Under Pressure

Remaining calm in the face of disruptions is a skill that can be cultivated. Practice these techniques:

- **Breathing and Grounding Exercises**: Take deep, steady
  breaths to center yourself. Visualize a fixed point in the room
  to anchor your focus and regain composure.

- **Affirmations**: Silently repeat phrases like, *"I'm in control,
  and I can handle this."*

- These affirmations reinforce your confidence at the moment. Confidence is cultivated not just through practice but
  also through embracing vulnerability. Consider using affirmations, visualizing success, and reflecting on your past accomplishments as tools to boost self-assurance. When practiced consistently, these habits create a foundation of unwavering confidence.

- **Rehearse Responses**: Anticipate tough questions or challenging comments and prepare concise, respectful replies.
  Practicing these responses builds resilience, helping you navigate disruptions with ease.

Turning Disruptions into Opportunities

Disruptions don't have to derail your presentation—they can become
moments of connection.

- **Incorporate Humor**: A light-hearted comment or
  well-timed joke can diffuse tension and re-engage your audience. For example: *"Looks like we've got some lively debate*

*going on—just the kind of energy we need!"*Shared laughter can create camaraderie and bring the focus back to your message.

- **Reinforce Key Points**: Use interruptions as opportunities to elaborate. If someone questions a concept, integrate their comment into your narrative to deepen understanding and reinforce your message.

By handling disruptions with adaptability and confidence, you demonstrate poise and professionalism—qualities that leave a lasting impression on your audience. Confidence is cultivated not just in practice but also in embracing vulnerability. Consider using affirmations, visualizing success, and reflecting on your past accomplishments as tools to boost self-assurance.

Pauses and disruptions, when approached strategically, can enhance your presentation and strengthen your connection with your audience. By practicing pauses and handling disruptions with grace, you turn potential obstacles into opportunities to engage, connect, and inspire.

4.7 Cultivating a Dynamic Speaking Presence

Imagine stepping onto the stage, the energy in the room buzzing with anticipation. Your goal isn't merely to deliver information but to captivate—to connect with your audience in a way that leaves a lasting impression. Developing a strong speaking presence is the key to achieving this. It's a combination of body language, vocal mastery, eye contact, and thorough preparation that transforms a presentation into a memorable experience.

Body Language: Projecting Confidence and Openness

Confidence is cultivated not just in practice but also in embracing vulnerability. Consider using affirmations, visualizing success, and reflecting on your past accomplishments as tools to boost self-assurance.

Your body language speaks volumes before you even utter a word. **Open and welcoming gestures** invite your audience to engage with you, creating an immediate connection.

- A simple movement of your hands can emphasize a point, making it more memorable.

- Expansive gestures project confidence, signaling that you are comfortable and in control. Confidence is cultivated not just in practice but also in embracing vulnerability. Consider using affirmations, visualizing success, and reflecting on your past accomplishments as tools to boost self-assurance.

This openness encourages your audience to relax and lowers their defenses, making them more receptive to your message. However, it's important to strike a balance—subtle, purposeful movements are often more powerful than overly exaggerated gestures. By aligning your body language with your message, you reinforce your points and maintain a commanding presence.

Vocal Variety: Keeping Your Audience Engaged

Your voice is one of your most powerful tools for capturing and maintaining attention. **Vocal variety** adds dynamism to your delivery, transforming a presentation from monotonous to captivating.

- Use softer tones to draw your audience in, encouraging them to lean forward and listen closely.

- Raise your volume at key moments to emphasize critical points and ensure they stick.

- Strategic pauses add weight to your words, giving your audience time to absorb and reflect.

Emphasizing key phrases or words further enhances your message, making it unforgettable. By mastering these vocal techniques, you create a dynamic listening experience that keeps your audience engaged and your message impactful.

Eye Contact: Building Rapport and Connection

Eye contact is vital to building rapport. It creates a personal connection with your audience, making each person feel seen and valued.

- As you scan the room, make deliberate eye contact with individuals. This technique not only engages those you connect with but also creates the illusion of speaking directly to each person in the room.

- Balance eye contact with glances at your notes to maintain both connection and structure.

When your audience feels acknowledged, they're more likely to engage with your message. This shared experience deepens their connection to your narrative, creating a sense of collaboration and trust.

Preparation: The Foundation of Confidence

Confidence on stage is built long before you step onto it. **Thorough preparation** lays the groundwork for a dynamic speaking presence. Confidence is cultivated not just in practice but also in embracing vulnerability. Consider using affirmations, visualizing success, and reflecting on your past accomplishments as tools to boost self-assurance.

- **Rehearsal Techniques**: Practice your presentation multiple times, focusing on both content and delivery. Repetition builds familiarity, reduces anxiety, and boosts confidence. True confidence is built through both preparation and stepping outside your comfort zone.However, it is achieved not just in practice but also in embracing vulnerability. Consider using affirmations, visualizing success, and reflecting on your past accomplishments as tools to boost self-assurance.

- **Visualization**: Mentally rehearse your presentation. Imagine the room, the audience, and your confident delivery. Visualizing success primes your mind, making the real experience feel familiar and manageable.

With solid preparation, you step onto the stage with assurance, ready to engage and inspire your audience.

4.8 The Power of Presence

A dynamic speaking presence is about more than words—it's about how you carry yourself, use your voice, and connect with your audience. These elements converge to create a presentation that resonates far beyond the final applause.

Your presence is your most powerful tool. By honing your body language, voice, eye contact, and preparation, you elevate your message and ensure it reaches and impacts your audience meaningfully.

Over time, as you refine these skills, you'll transcend being just a speaker—you'll become a communicator who captivates, inspires, and leaves a lasting impression.

Audience engagement goes beyond merely holding attention—it's about fostering an interactive and collaborative experience that deeply connects. By employing interactive techniques, embracing technology, and cultivating a commanding presence, you transform your presentation into a dynamic dialogue. This approach ensures your message resonates long after the final word has been spoken.

Chapter Five

Preparation and Practice

Picture this: you're in the middle of a hectic workweek, juggling meetings, deadlines, and personal commitments when you're tasked with preparing for an upcoming presentation. The prospect can feel overwhelming, but with the right strategies, preparation doesn't have to be stressful. This chapter focuses on how to manage your time effectively and integrate preparation seamlessly into your busy schedule.

By finding a rhythm that aligns with your professional and personal life, you can prepare thoroughly without sacrificing balance. Through prioritization, practical scheduling, and productivity tools, you can turn preparation from a daunting chore into an efficient and manageable routine.

Prioritizing Your Speech Preparation Tasks

The first step to efficient preparation is prioritizing your tasks. Start by identifying the key components of your preparation, such as:

- Researching your topic.

- Drafting your speech.

- Rehearsing your delivery.

Create a **task hierarchy**, ordering tasks by importance and urgency. For instance, research might be the first priority, as it lays the foundation for your content, while rehearsal comes later but remains essential.

Time-blocking methods are invaluable in managing these tasks. Allocate specific time slots for each activity to prevent your schedule from becoming overwhelming. For example:

- Dedicate Monday morning to research.

- Use Tuesday afternoon to outline your key points.

- Set aside Wednesday evening for a preliminary rehearsal.

This structured approach keeps you on track, minimizes procrastination, and ensures steady progress toward a polished presentation.

Creating a Practical Preparation Schedule

A well-structured schedule is essential for staying on top of your preparation while balancing other responsibilities.

- **Set Realistic Deadlines**: Break down your overall timeline into manageable chunks. Assign deadlines for individual tasks, such as completing research by a specific date or finalizing your slides by the end of the week.

- **Block Time in Your Calendar**: Treat preparation sessions as non-negotiable appointments. Allocate specific time slots for each task and stick to them.

- **Be Flexible but Disciplined**: Life happens, so adjust your schedule as needed. However, maintain a disciplined approach to ensure consistent progress.

A planned schedule reduces last-minute rushes and instills confidence, knowing you've dedicated sufficient time to every aspect of your presentation. Confidence is cultivated not just in practice but also in embracing vulnerability. Consider using affirmations, visualizing success, and reflecting on your past accomplishments as tools to boost self-assurance.

Leveraging Productivity Tools

Productivity tools can streamline your preparation, making the process both efficient and effective. Consider these options:

- **Digital Calendars and Reminders**: Use tools like Google Calendar or Microsoft Outlook to schedule preparation tasks and set reminders.

- **Task Management Apps**: Platforms like **Trello** or **Asana** help you organize and track your progress.

  - **Trello's visual boards** are particularly useful for breaking tasks into smaller steps, setting deadlines, and monitoring your achievements.

- ○ **Asana**'s collaborative features are great if you're working on group presentations.

By leveraging these tools, you enhance productivity and eliminate the distractions of disorganization, allowing you to focus fully on your preparation.

Balancing Preparation with Other Responsibilities

For busy professionals, balancing preparation with daily obligations is crucial. Integrate preparation into your routine by combining it with existing activities:

- **Listen to Podcasts or Audiobooks**: Use your commute or workout time to consume relevant content related to your presentation.

- **Brainstorm During Breaks**: Use lunch breaks or short downtime periods to jot down ideas or refine your outline.

This multitasking approach maximizes your time while maintaining balance, ensuring that preparation doesn't overshadow other commitments.

By weaving preparation into your daily life, you create a sustainable routine that supports both your professional and personal goals.

Time-Blocking Exercise

1. **Set Up Your Schedule**: Use a digital calendar or task management app to create a weekly schedule. Identify key preparation tasks such as research, drafting, and rehearsing.

2. **Allocate Time Blocks**: Assign specific time blocks for each task, considering your peak productivity times. For example:

   ○ Research: Monday morning when the focus is sharp.

   ○ Rehearsal: Evenings, to simulate post-work presentation energy.

3. **Review and Adjust**: At the end of the week, review your schedule. Were you able to stick to your time blocks? Identify areas where adjustments are needed.

This exercise helps you create a personalized routine that aligns with your unique needs. It boosts efficiency and reduces stress during the preparation process.

Conclusion

Preparation doesn't have to be overwhelming, even for busy professionals. By prioritizing tasks, scheduling effectively, and leveraging productivity tools, you can create an efficient routine that integrates seamlessly into your life. Balancing preparation with your other responsibilities ensures you approach each presentation with confidence and clarity, all while maintaining harmony in your schedule. Confidence is cultivated not just in practice but also in embracing vulnerability. Practicing visualization and positive reinforcement can enhance your sense of self-assurance

This chapter equips you with the strategies to prepare efficiently, helping you focus on what matters most: delivering a presentation that informs, inspires, and connects.

5.2 Rehearsal Techniques for Maximum Retention

Rehearsal is more than repetition—it's about refining your delivery, boosting your confidence, and ensuring your message resonates. Here are techniques to maximize retention and impact: True confidence is built through both preparation and stepping outside your comfort zone.

Mirror Practice: Dual Perspectives

Practicing in front of a mirror engages multiple senses, enhancing both retention and self-awareness.

- **Observe Your Body Language**: As you speak, watch your gestures and posture. Are they open and confident? Adjust as needed to reinforce your message.

- **Facial Expressions**: Ensure your expressions match your tone and content, adding authenticity and emotional resonance.

Mirror practice grounds you in the moment, preparing you to face your audience with poise and confidence.

Recording for Feedback

Recording your speech—audio or video—provides invaluable insights into your delivery.

- **Review Your Performance**: Play back the recording to assess vocal clarity, pacing, and emphasis. Are you rushing? Are your pauses effective?

- **Seek Constructive Feedback**: Share recordings with trusted colleagues who can provide objective insights. Their perspectives can highlight areas for improvement, helping you refine both content and delivery.

While reviewing recordings can feel uncomfortable, it's one of the most effective ways to polish your presentation.

Simulating Real-World Conditions

Rehearsing under conditions that mimic your actual presentation environment can significantly reduce anxiety.

- **Recreate the Venue**: Practice in a setting similar to your presentation space, paying attention to acoustics and lighting.

- **Time Constraints**: Use a timer to ensure you stay within your allotted time while maintaining clarity and engagement.

This strategy familiarizes you with the environment and conditions, building confidence and readiness for the real event.

Varied Rehearsal Formats

Keep your practice dynamic by incorporating different rehearsal techniques:

- **Alternate Between Scripted and Impromptu Practice**: Reading your script helps internalize content, while impromptu speaking builds adaptability.

- **Role-Playing Audience Interactions**: Enlist a friend or colleague to simulate audience questions. This prepares you to handle interruptions and unexpected challenges confidently.

These varied formats ensure you approach your presentation from multiple angles, enhancing both adaptability and mastery.

Interactive Feedback Exercise

Organize a mock presentation session with a small group of peers:
1. Deliver your speech as if it were the real presentation.

2. Invite your peers to provide feedback on your content, delivery, and engagement.

3. Encourage them to ask questions, simulating audience interactions.

This exercise sharpens your presentation skills and exposes you to diverse perspectives, boosting confidence and refining your delivery.

Conclusion

Rehearsal isn't just about practicing—it's about preparing to connect, engage, and inspire. By integrating mirror practice, recording, real-world simulation, and interactive feedback into your preparation, you equip yourself with the tools to deliver a compelling and adaptable performance. These techniques ensure that when the moment comes, you'll stand before your audience with confidence and clarity.

5.3 Crafting Elevator Pitches: The Art of Brevity

Picture yourself in a crowded elevator, the doors about to close. You have just one minute to make an unforgettable impression. This is the essence of an **elevator pitch**—a concise, impactful summary of who you are and what you stand for.

At its core, a powerful elevator pitch relies on clear, concise messaging. It's about cutting through the noise and delivering your essence in a way that's both memorable and compelling. Start with a **compelling hook**—a statement or question that grabs attention and sets the tone for your pitch. This hook is your golden ticket, sparking curiosity and prompting further conversation.

Developing a Personal Pitch Template

Creating a flexible, adaptable **personal pitch template** is a game-changer. This template provides a foundation for quick yet effective pitches tailored to different contexts and audiences.

- **Identify Key Points**: What are the core messages you want to communicate? Highlight your unique selling propositions—the qualities or experiences that set you apart.

- **Understand Your Audience**: What do they need to know about you? Consider what will resonate most with their needs and interests.

- **Structure Your Pitch**: Organize your message into three clear parts:

    a. **Introduction**: Start with your name and role or area of expertise.

b. **Core Message**: Offer a concise summary of what you do and why it matters.

c. **Call to Action**: End with a statement or question that encourages further engagement.

With a solid template in hand, you can quickly adapt your pitch to suit various scenarios, whether it's a networking event, a casual introduction, or a professional meeting.

Practicing Pitch Delivery

Crafting the pitch is only half the battle—delivery is what brings it to life.

- **Modulate Your Voice**: Emphasize key points to create a dynamic and engaging rhythm. Let your tone convey enthusiasm, confidence, and authority, ensuring your message stands out.

- **Use Body Language**: Align your physical presence with your verbal message. Gestures can reinforce key points, while a smile conveys approachability and warmth. Maintain **eye contact** to build trust and connection.

- **Rehearse for Natural Delivery**: Practice your pitch repeatedly until it feels effortless. Confidence comes from familiarity, so the more you rehearse, the easier it becomes to deliver your pitch in any setting.

Adapting Pitches to Diverse Audiences

Every audience is unique, with distinct needs and expectations. Adapting your pitch to suit different listeners is essential for maximizing its impact.

- **Tailor Your Language**: For technical audiences, use industry-specific terms that demonstrate expertise. For general audiences, opt for clear, straightforward language.

- **Highlight Relevant Benefits**: Focus on what's most meaningful to the audience. Show them the value you bring in terms they understand and appreciate.

This customization shows awareness and respect for your audience's perspective, enhancing your pitch's effectiveness and ensuring your message resonates.

Conclusion

An elevator pitch is more than just words—it's a tool that can open doors, spark interest, and lay the groundwork for meaningful connections. By mastering the art of crafting and delivering concise, adaptable pitches, you amplify your professional presence and ensure your message makes a lasting impact.

5.4 Overcoming Last-Minute Hurdles

In the world of public speaking, last-minute hurdles are inevitable. Plans may change, content may need adjusting, or technical issues may arise, making adaptability a crucial skill. The key to navigating these challenges lies in preparation, composure, and flexibility. With the right strategies, you can turn potential obstacles into opportunities to showcase resilience and poise.

Prioritizing Core Messages

When unexpected disruptions occur, a well-thought-out **contingency plan** becomes your first line of defense. Start by identifying the **essential components** of your presentation:

- What's non-negotiable?

- Which core messages must be communicated no matter what happens?

By prioritizing these elements, you ensure that your key points remain intact even in the face of change. This clarity allows you to pivot easily, focusing on effectively delivering your core message. **Flexibility** is your ally, enabling you to adapt without losing sight of what truly matters.

Maintaining Composure Under Pressure

Your ability to remain composed in high-pressure situations can make all the difference.

1. **Breathing and Grounding Exercises**:

   ○ Take slow, deliberate breaths: inhale through your nose, hold for a count of three, and exhale through your mouth. This simple technique calms nerves and clears your mind, preparing you to think clearly.

2. **Positive Self-Talk**:

   ○ Replace thoughts like *"This is a disaster"* with empowering affirmations such as *"I'm adapting and showing resilience.*"

- ○ Cognitive reframing, inspired by **Cognitive Behavioral Therapy (CBT),** shifts your mindset from panic to problem-solving, helping you stay focused and confident.

With these techniques, you can turn a potentially chaotic situation into a moment of controlled adaptability.

Leveraging Improvisational Skills

Improvisation is more than spontaneity—it's about being prepared to think on your feet and respond effectively.

- **Practice Impromptu Speaking**:

  - ○ Set aside time for exercises that challenge your quick-thinking abilities. For example, choose a random topic and speak about it for one minute, focusing on coherence and clarity.

  - ○ This practice sharpens your ability to respond to unexpected questions or disruptions.

- **Stay Agile**:

  - ○ When a hurdle arises, use your adaptability to pivot gracefully. Improvisational skills allow you to maintain the flow of your presentation, demonstrating both confidence and control.

Ensuring Technical Readiness

Technical glitches can derail even the most polished presentations, so preparation is essential.

- **Test Equipment in Advance**

- : Arrive early to familiarize yourself with the venue's technology. Test the microphone, projector, and lighting to ensure everything functions properly. Emerging technologies like virtual and augmented reality are also reshaping how audiences interact with presentations. By experimenting with these tools, speakers can create immersive experiences that go beyond traditional slides and visuals. When used thoughtfully, such innovations can leave a lasting impact.

- **Have Backups**:

    ○ Bring a USB drive with your presentation and a printed copy of your notes.

    ○ Keep spare batteries or an alternative clicker on hand if you're using a remote device.

By anticipating potential technical challenges, you create a safety net that minimizes disruptions and keeps your presentation on track.

Conclusion

Last-minute hurdles don't have to derail your presentation. By prioritizing core messages, staying composed under pressure, leveraging improvisational skills, and ensuring technical readiness, you can navigate unexpected challenges with confidence. These strategies not only keep your presentation intact but also showcase your resilience and professionalism. With preparation and adaptability, you'll turn potential obstacles into opportunities to connect, inspire, and leave a lasting impression.

5.5 Practicing with Tech: Leveraging Digital Tools

In today's digital age, technology offers a wide range of tools to enhance your public speaking practice, making preparation more efficient, engaging, and precise. From speech analysis apps to virtual reality simulations, these tools empower you to refine your skills, gain confidence, and excel in any speaking scenario. Emerging technologies like virtual and augmented reality are also reshaping how audiences interact with presentations. By experimenting with these tools, speakers can create immersive experiences that go beyond traditional slides and visuals. Such innovations can leave a lasting impact when used thoughtfully.

Speech Analysis Apps: Data-Driven Feedback

Speech analysis apps provide immediate, actionable feedback on your delivery.

- **Key Features**: These apps analyze metrics like pace, volume, clarity, and even filler word usage.

- **Benefits**: By identifying specific areas for improvement, you can focus on refining your performance with precision.

For instance, if an app indicates that your pace is too fast, you can adjust accordingly in subsequent practice sessions. This data-driven approach ensures that every session is productive, helping you build confidence and clarity.

Virtual Platforms: Remote Practice and Feedback

Virtual platforms such as **Zoom** and **Google Meet** open up opportunities for remote practice:

- **Rehearse with a Remote Audience**: Connect with colleagues, mentors, or peers who can provide real-time feedback.

- **Simulate Online Presentations**: Practice navigating virtual settings, including managing screen sharing and audience engagement.

Proficiency in virtual presentations is essential in today's workplace. By practicing in this environment, you will become familiar with and confident in handling online speaking engagements professionally and easily.

Virtual Reality (VR): Immersive Rehearsal

Virtual reality takes practice to a new level, simulating real-world speaking environments.

- **Simulated Environments**: Practice in settings ranging from small meetings to large conferences, immersing yourself in the sensations of a live audience.

- **Anxiety Management**: Exposure to realistic scenarios helps reduce speaking anxiety, building confidence over time.

- **Audience Interaction**: VR platforms often include simulated audience feedback, allowing you to practice responding to visual cues, questions, or applause.

By incorporating VR into your routine, you prepare for high-stakes presentations in a controlled, realistic setting.

CBT-Inspired Gradual Exposure Techniques

Gradual exposure, inspired by **Cognitive Behavioral Therapy (CBT),** helps ease the transition into public speaking:

1. **Start Small**: Begin by recording yourself presenting to a small online audience.

2. **Review Critically**: Watch the recording, noting areas for improvement.

3. **Expand Your Audience**: Gradually increase the size of your audience as your confidence grows.

This step-by-step approach helps you build comfort and control, making larger presentations feel manageable and natural.

Recording and Playback for Self-Assessment

Recording your practice sessions is one of the most effective self-assessment tools:

- **Video Recordings**: Observe your body language, identifying gestures or habits that may distract from your message.

- **Audio Recordings**: To ensure a clear and engaging delivery, focus on vocal clarity, tone, and pacing.

This process of recording and playback allows you to fine-tune your performance and align it with your goals.

Online Speaking Communities: Collaborative Growth

Engaging with online speaking communities provides a supportive environment for development:

- **Peer Feedback**: Participate in forums or groups dedicated to public speaking to gain constructive feedback and shared experiences.

- **Virtual Practice Sessions**: Join group sessions to practice with diverse audiences and receive critiques from multiple perspectives.

This collaborative approach enriches your understanding of effective communication strategies while boosting your confidence.

Conclusion

Technology has transformed the way we prepare for public speaking, offering innovative tools to refine our skills and build confidence. From speech analysis apps and virtual platforms to VR simulations and online communities, leveraging these resources equips you to engage, inform, and inspire with greater impact. By integrating these tools into your routine, you set the stage for success in any speaking scenario. Emerging technologies like virtual and augmented reality are also reshaping how audiences interact with presentations. By experimenting with these tools, speakers can create immersive experiences that go beyond traditional slides and visuals. Such innovations can leave a lasting impact when used thoughtfully.

This chapter has equipped you with the tools to navigate the intricacies of cultural communication, preparing you for the rich and rewarding interactions that lie ahead. As we move forward, let's build on these insights to strengthen our connections and amplify our influence in the global arena.

Congratulations on Reaching This Milestone!
You're halfway through your journey to public speaking mastery—well done!

Are You Finding Value So Far? Let Us Know!

Hi there! If this book has sparked ideas, given you an "aha!" moment, or helped you feel more confident so far, I'd love to hear about it.

Your feedback doesn't just mean the world to me—it helps future readers like you. What you share could inspire someone else to pick up this book and start their own journey toward confident communication.

Take a quick moment to share your thoughts here:
https://www.amazon.com/review/review-your-purchases/?asin=

Thank you for being part of this journey! Keep up the great work as you continue to master public speaking.

Chapter Six

Confidence Building: Strategies for Lasting Assurance

Confidence is cultivated not just in practice but also in embracing vulnerability. Consider using affirmations, visualizing success, and reflecting on your past accomplishments as tools to boost self-assurance. These habits, when practiced consistently, create a foundation of unwavering confidence.

Consider the moment just before stepping onto the stage. The anticipation is like standing at the edge of a diving board, ready to leap into the unknown. Confidence is your springboard, and building it requires a mix of personalized exercises and daily rituals. It begins with understanding your unique strengths and challenges and crafting a plan that turns fear into fuel. Imagine the power of entering a room and feeling assured—not because you're fearless, but because you've transformed that fear into energy and focus.

6.1 Designing Personalized Confidence Exercises

Building confidence begins with identifying the triggers behind your anxiety. Is it the fear of forgetting your lines or the worry of being judged by your audience? Pinpointing these triggers allows you to address them directly. .

- **Targeted Exercises:**

    - If you fear forgetting your speech, practice delivering it in front of a mirror or with a small, supportive group. This builds familiarity and reduces the fear of the unknown.

    - If you are concerned about audience judgment, seek feedback from trusted colleagues. Constructive insights can help you refine your approach, turning feedback into a tool for growth instead of a source of anxiety.

Tailored exercises empower you to focus on your strengths while proactively addressing challenges, making confidence a skill you build step by step.

Incorporating Daily Confidence Rituals

- **Morning Affirmations:** Begin your day with positive statements like, *"I've prepared well, and I'm ready."* Focus on effort and preparation rather than perfection. These affirmations reinforce your strengths and foster a sense of control.

- **Power Poses:** Stand tall, shoulders back, and take deep breaths before your presentation. This posture not only boosts confidence but also reduces stress. Research shows that power poses can increase testosterone levels and decrease cortisol, improving your readiness to perform. **Confidence Journaling:** Dedicate a journal to tracking affirmations, progress, and victories—no matter how small. Reviewing these entries reminds you of your growth and solidifies your belief in your abilities.

These rituals create a foundation for consistent self-assurance, allowing you to start each day with clarity and determination.

Building Confidence Through Skill Mastery

- **Vocal Projection:** Practice speaking from your diaphragm rather than your throat to achieve a clear, confident voice. Strong vocal projection not only conveys authority but also ensures your message is heard.

- **Memorable Openings and Closings:** Craft compelling opening and closing statements. A strong opening captures your audience's attention, while a powerful closing ensures your message lingers in their minds. Practice these sections until they feel natural and impactful.

Honing these skills builds confidence by equipping you with tools to communicate effectively. The more prepared you are, the more assured you'll feel.

Tracking Progress and Celebrating Wins

- **Maintain a Confidence Journal:** Record your experiences, reflections, and milestones. Document small victories, such as speaking without notes or engaging the audience with a thoughtful question.

- **Set Incremental Goals:** Break down your objectives into manageable steps. For example, aim to speak for a certain duration or deliver a talk with a specific focus.

- **Celebrate Achievements:** Recognize every step forward, no matter how small. Rewards can be as simple as savoring a treat or reflecting on your effort with pride. This positive reinforcement fosters growth and motivates you to continue improving.

Tracking progress helps reinforce the belief that you're capable and steadily improving. Each milestone is a testament to your growth, propelling you toward greater confidence and success in your speaking endeavors.

Conclusion

Confidence isn't about being perfect—it's about being prepared. By designing personalized exercises, incorporating daily rituals, mastering key skills, and celebrating progress, you transform speaking anxiety into an assured presence. These practices lay the groundwork for lasting confidence, allowing you to approach public speaking not with fear but with purpose and poise.

6.2 Developing a Growth Mindset for Public Speaking

Imagine approaching public speaking not as a daunting hurdle but as an opportunity for continuous growth and development. This shift in perspective is rooted in the **growth mindset**—the belief that abilities can be cultivated through effort, learning, and perseverance. Embracing challenges as opportunities for improvement is at the heart of this approach. By viewing each speaking engagement as a chance to refine your skills, you replace fear with curiosity. Criticism becomes a valuable tool for growth rather than a personal affront.

Adopting a growth mindset involves embracing feedback as guidance toward becoming a more effective communicator. Cognitive Behavioral Therapy (CBT) techniques can be particularly helpful in challenging self-limiting beliefs. If you find yourself thinking, *"I'll never be good at public speaking,"* reframe it as *"I'm improving with every practice session."* This subtle shift fosters resilience and progression. Keeping a journal of small wins and moments of growth further reinforces this outlook. Each entry serves as a testament to your progress, boosting both confidence and commitment to continuous improvement.

6.3 Reframing Failure as a Stepping Stone

Viewing failure through a growth lens transforms it from a source of fear into a powerful learning tool. Analyze past speaking experiences—not to dwell on mistakes, but to uncover lessons. Ask yourself:

- What went well?

- What areas could be improved?

These reflections provide a roadmap for setting new goals. After a setback, resist the urge to focus solely on what went wrong. Instead, consider how you can apply those lessons to future presentations. This proactive mindset encourages risk-taking and opens the door to new opportunities. By understanding failure as an integral part of the learning process, you cultivate resilience and adaptability, essential qualities for thriving in public speaking.

Building Resilience and Perseverance

Resilience is the foundation for navigating the ups and downs of public speaking. Surround yourself with a supportive network or community that encourages growth and offers constructive feedback. Engaging with like-minded individuals who share your commitment to improvement can provide motivation and fresh insights. These connections create a safe space to share experiences, celebrate successes, and learn from challenges.

Self-compassion and patience are equally important. Recognize that mastery takes time, and allow yourself the grace to progress at your own pace. Celebrate small victories along the way, focusing on progress rather than perfection. Embracing the journey with kindness toward yourself fosters the confidence to keep improving, one step at a time.

Commitment to Lifelong Learning

A growth mindset thrives on continuous learning. Stay engaged with resources that expand your knowledge and sharpen your skills:

- **Workshops and Seminars:** Attend events that provide new insights, techniques, and opportunities to connect with experienced speakers.

- **Public Speaking Media:** Explore books, podcasts, and videos to gain diverse perspectives and strategies you can incorporate into your practice.

This commitment to ongoing development ensures your approach remains fresh and adaptable, preparing you to meet the evolving demands of public speaking with confidence and competence.

Conclusion

By developing a growth mindset, you turn public speaking into an opportunity for continuous improvement and self-discovery. Each engagement becomes a stepping stone toward mastery, driven by your willingness to learn, adapt, and persevere. Through reframing failure, building resilience, and embracing lifelong learning, you cultivate the confidence to face challenges head-on, transforming obstacles into opportunities for growth.

6.4 The Feedback Loop: Using Critiques to Improve

Picture this: you've just finished a presentation. The adrenaline is still coursing through your veins, and a mix of relief and curiosity lingers. Was your message well-received? What could you have done differently? This is where feedback becomes invaluable. Think of it as a compass, offering guidance for your growth and helping you navigate areas that might not be apparent from your own perspective.

However, not all feedback is created equal. Differentiating between **constructive** and **destructive** feedback is essential. Constructive feedback is specific, actionable, and growth-oriented. It highlights your strengths while offering clear suggestions for improvement. Destructive feedback, on the other hand, is often vague, negative, and unproductive, providing little guidance for change. To truly benefit, seek feedback from diverse sources—mentors, colleagues, and even your audience. These varied perspectives enrich your understanding and provide a more comprehensive view of your performance.

Building a Feedback Network

Creating a feedback network is an investment in your development. Start by identifying individuals who understand your goals and are committed to supporting your growth. These people should offer honest, constructive insights that are both candid and supportive.

- **Establish a Feedback Routine:** Schedule regular opportunities for feedback, such as a debrief after each presentation or periodic check-ins with your mentors.

- **Diverse Perspectives:** Include voices from different roles—peers who can relate to your experience, mentors with seasoned advice, and audience members who represent the end recipient of your message.

Regular feedback fosters a culture of continuous improvement. It shifts the process of learning from sporadic occurrences to an ongoing journey, keeping you accountable, engaged, and consistently progressing.

Analyzing and Integrating Feedback

Once feedback is received, the real work begins: analyzing and integrating it effectively.

- **Look for Patterns:** Are there recurring themes or suggestions? These patterns often point to areas of improvement and consistent strengths.

- **Turn Criticism into Action:** Use constructive feedback as a roadmap for growth. For instance, if you're advised to work on vocal projection, incorporate breathing exercises and voice modulation techniques into your preparation. If your audience engagement is lacking, experiment with more interactive storytelling or Q&A sessions. Storytelling serves as the bridge between facts and emotions, allowing the audience to visualize and internalize the message. Adding a vivid description or a relatable personal anecdote can make the message even more memorable. Think of a moment when a story changed your perspective—it is this transformation that storytelling brings to public speaking.

- **Focus on Incremental Growth:** Small, actionable changes compound over time, leading to noticeable improvements in your delivery and content.

Feedback isn't just about identifying weaknesses; it's about leveraging insights to enhance your strengths and refine your performance.

Balancing Feedback with Self-Assessment

While external feedback is valuable, self-assessment provides crucial context and fosters self-awareness.

- **Self-Reflection Journal:** After each presentation, document your reflections:

    - What went well?

    - What challenges did you face?

    - What areas could be improved?

- **Compare Insights:** Cross-reference your self-assessment with external feedback. This alignment (or discrepancy) deepens your understanding of your performance, highlighting blind spots and validating your strengths.

Balancing external critiques with personal reflection creates a holistic view of your progress. It helps you recognize patterns, contextualize feedback, and prioritize areas for improvement.

The Feedback Loop in Action

The feedback loop is a continuous cycle of **receiving, analyzing**, and **integrating** feedback enriched by self-reflection.

1. **Receive Feedback:** Actively seek constructive critiques from diverse sources.

2. **Analyze Feedback:** Identify patterns and actionable insights.

3. **Integrate Feedback:** Make targeted adjustments to refine your performance.

4. **Reflect Personally:** Combine feedback with your own observations for a well-rounded perspective.

This dynamic process evolves with you, equipping you with the insights needed to navigate the complexities of public speaking. By embracing feedback, you open yourself to new ideas, perspectives, and strategies, continuously refining your skills and building the confidence to speak with authority and impact.

Conclusion

Every piece of feedback—whether positive or critical—is an opportunity for growth. By learning to embrace and leverage critiques, you transform them into tools for continuous improvement. The feedback loop shapes you into a more effective, self-aware, and confident communicator, capable of delivering messages that resonate with clarity and conviction.

6.5 Embracing Mistakes: Learning from Every Experience

Mistakes are inevitable. They're an intrinsic part of the human experience, particularly in public speaking. However, viewing them as failures can stifle growth. Instead, recognize mistakes as valuable opportunities for learning. Each misstep highlights areas that need improvement. Analyzing what went wrong provides actionable insights that guide future success.

Forgot a key point? Stumbled over your words? Rather than dwelling on the error, ask yourself, *What did this teach me?* Shifting your perspective reframes mistakes as stepping stones for growth. This positive mindset fosters resilience, enabling you to approach future speaking engagements with renewed confidence and assurance.

Recovering Gracefully During Presentations

Handling mistakes with poise ensures you maintain credibility. The way you respond to errors often matters more than the mistake itself.

- **Quick Recovery Phrases:** If you lose your train of thought, use phrases like, *"Let's dive deeper into that,"* to give yourself a moment to regroup. If you misstated a fact, address it transparently: *"Correction, what I meant to say was..."* This honesty strengthens your audience's trust.

- **Using Humor Effectively:** Light-heartedly acknowledging a slip-up can diffuse tension and turn a setback into a moment of connection. A shared laugh over a minor error can relax both you and your audience, transforming an awkward moment into an opportunity for engagement.

These strategies ensure that even you maintain control, confidence, and composure when things don't go as planned.

Incorporating Mistakes into Your Stories

Mistakes aren't just learning moments—they can enrich your storytelling. Sharing personal errors adds depth, relatability, and authenticity to your narrative. Storytelling serves as the bridge between facts and emotions, allowing the audience to visualize and internalize the message. Adding a vivid description or a relatable personal anecdote can make the message even more memorable. Think of a moment when a story changed your perspective—it is this transformation that storytelling brings to public speaking.

- **Humanizing Your Experiences:** Reflect on past challenges and how you overcame them. For instance, if you underestimated the preparation time for a significant presentation, recounting that experience—and how you adapted—can resonate with your audience.

- **Offering Valuable Lessons:** By openly discussing the lessons learned, you provide actionable insights for others. Your mistakes become an opportunity to connect, showing your audience that growth often arises from setbacks.

Incorporating these moments into your speeches creates narratives that are both genuine and engaging, fostering empathy and connection with your listeners.

Creating a Culture of Learning from Mistakes

A supportive environment is essential for normalizing and learning from mistakes.

- **Sharing Experiences with Peers:** Discuss challenges and setbacks openly with colleagues or team members. This collective approach not only provides valuable insights but also normalizes mistakes as a natural part of the learning process.

- **Fostering Open Dialogue:** Encourage discussions about what went wrong and brainstorm ways to improve. This openness not only accelerates personal growth but also strengthens team dynamics, turning individual learning into shared development.

By embracing a culture that values lessons from mistakes, you reduce the fear of failure and foster a mindset of continuous improvement.

Mistakes as a Catalyst for Growth

Mistakes are not the end; they're the beginning. They represent your willingness to step out of your comfort zone and strive for growth. Each error is a lesson learned, a skill sharpened, and a reminder that perfection is not the goal—progress is.

- **Developing Resilience:** Analyzing mistakes teaches you how to adapt and improve, building resilience and confidence.

- **Sharpening Competence:** Every misstep contributes to your development, preparing you to engage and connect with audiences more effectively.

Mistakes are not roadblocks; they are guideposts on your journey to becoming a more authentic, relatable, and impactful communicator.

Conclusion

Confidence in public speaking isn't about avoiding mistakes; it's about embracing them as opportunities to learn and grow. The insights gained from analyzing and addressing errors shape you into a more adaptable and capable speaker. Each lesson learned equips you with the tools to engage audiences authentically and effectively.

As we move forward, the next chapter delves into cultural sensitivity and global communication, equipping you to connect with diverse audiences and expand your reach as a speaker. Adopting a mindset of global awareness enriches your communication. Being open to learning about traditions, social cues, and language nuances allows for deeper connections. By engaging with diverse groups, you gain insights that shape your message to resonate universally.

Chapter Seven

Cultural Sensitivity and Global Communication

Adopting a mindset of global awareness enriches communication. Being open to learning about traditions, social cues, and language nuances allows for deeper connections. Engaging with diverse groups gives you insights that shape your message to resonate universally.

Imagine you're at an international conference, surrounded by professionals from every corner of the globe. Conversations fill the room, each voice carrying the rhythm of its native tongue, each face animated with expressions unique to their cultural backgrounds. As you engage with these diverse minds, the significance of understanding the subtleties of communication across cultures becomes evident. This awareness is not merely a courtesy; it's a critical component of effective interaction and successful presentations. Misunderstandings stemming from cultural differences can arise, but these moments also offer opportunities for growth, learning, and connection. In today's increasingly globalized world, navigating these cultural nuances is essential for meaningful communication.

Recognizing Cultural Communication Styles

Understanding cultural communication styles is the first step toward bridging gaps with diverse audiences. Anthropologist Edward T. Hall's framework of **high-context** and **low-context cultures** illustrates how societies convey meaning differently:

- **High-Context Cultures**: Found in regions like Japan, China, and Arab countries, these cultures rely heavily on non-verbal cues, shared understanding, and the surrounding context. Much of the meaning is implied rather than explicitly stated, and relationships and trust are paramount.

- **Low-Context Cultures**: These are common in countries like the United States and Germany; these cultures prioritize directness and clarity. Communication is explicit, with meaning embedded in the spoken or written word rather than the context of the interaction.

Tailoring your presentations to align with these styles ensures your message resonates, regardless of cultural background. For example, when addressing a high-context audience, emphasize storytelling and relational elements, while for a low-context audience, focus on clear, concise messaging with well-structured points. Storytelling serves as the bridge between facts and emotions, allowing the audience to visualize and internalize the message. Adding a vivid description or a relatable personal anecdote can make the message even more memorable. Think of a moment when a story changed your perspective—it is this transformation that storytelling brings to public speaking.

The Role of Non-Verbal Communication

Non-verbal communication often speaks louder than words, and its nuances vary significantly across cultures.

- **Eye Contact**: In Western cultures, maintaining eye contact signifies confidence and honesty, while in some Asian and Middle Eastern cultures, it can be perceived as confrontational or disrespectful.

- **Gestures**: Simple gestures like a thumbs-up or peace sign may convey positivity in some cultures but hold offensive meanings in others.

- **Body Language**: Posture, hand movements, and physical proximity all carry cultural significance. Psychologist David Matsumoto notes that non-verbal behavior is crucial for sharing intentions and emotions, even when language barriers exist.

By researching and practicing cultural non-verbal cues, you foster understanding and connection, ensuring your message transcends linguistic differences.

The Influence of Cultural Values and Beliefs

Cultural values shape communication styles and influence how messages are received.

- **Hierarchy and Respect**: In many Asian cultures, hierarchy is deeply ingrained. Communication may be indirect to maintain harmony and show respect for authority. For example, when addressing senior professionals, deferential language and tone are key.

- **Individualism vs. Collectivism**: Western cultures often emphasize individualism, encouraging open dialogue and direct communication. In contrast, collectivist cultures value group harmony and prefer collaborative, less confrontational exchanges.

Understanding these values helps you adapt your tone, structure, and delivery to meet the expectations of your audience, fostering trust and receptivity.

Preparing for Culturally Diverse Audiences

Researching cultural backgrounds is essential for effective communication with global audiences.

- **Cultural Intelligence Resources**: Use online databases, cultural guides, and books to familiarize yourself with your audience's customs, traditions, and communication styles.

- **Engage Cultural Consultants**: Local experts can provide nuanced insights that general research may overlook, offering tips on preferences and sensitivities specific to your audience.

- **Demonstrate Respect**: Thoughtful preparation not only

boosts your confidence but also shows your audience that you value their culture, paving the way for meaningful connections.

Cultural Communication Reflection Exercise

Reflect on a recent interaction with someone from a different cultural background:

1. **Observe Styles**: What communication styles did you notice? How did they differ from your own?

2. **Non-Verbal Cues**: Reflect on non-verbal elements such as gestures, eye contact, or tone. How did they influence the interaction?

3. **Moments of Clarity or Misunderstanding**: Identify moments where communication either succeeded or faltered.

4. **Lessons Learned**

5. : Use these reflections to pinpoint areas for improvement in your cultural sensitivity and communication skills. Adopting a mindset of global awareness enriches your communication. Being open to learning about traditions, social cues, and language nuances allows for deeper connections. Engaging with diverse groups allows you to gain insights that shape your message to resonate universally.

Consider keeping a journal to track these insights and apply them to future interactions. This practice will enhance your cultural awareness and empower you to connect effectively with diverse audiences.

Conclusion

Cultural sensitivity is more than an awareness of differences—it's an actionable commitment to adapting and connecting across boundaries. By recognizing communication styles, understanding cultural values, and preparing thoughtfully, you position yourself as an effective and empathetic communicator. Mastering these skills not only enriches your presentations but also fosters genuine connections that transcend cultural divides. Adopting a mindset of global awareness enriches your communication. Being open to learning about traditions, social cues, and language nuances allows for deeper connections. By engaging with diverse groups, you gain insights that shape your message to resonate universally.

Next, we'll explore the practical applications of active listening and audience adaptation, equipping you with tools to refine your communication skills further.

7.2 Adapting Your Message for Global Audiences

In global communication, customizing your message for cultural relevance is essential to ensure it resonates with diverse audiences. This requires delving into the values and preferences of your audience—understanding what motivates them and what they hold dear. For example, when addressing a culture that values community and collective success, frame your message around themes of teamwork and shared achievement. Use universally relatable examples that transcend cultural borders. Stories of human perseverance or innovation, for instance, tap into shared human experiences, enabling audiences from different backgrounds to connect with your message. By balancing the familiar with the new, you can bridge cultural divides and deliver a message that is accessible and impactful.

Humor and Anecdotes: Striking the Right Balance

Humor and anecdotes are powerful tools for engaging an audience but must be carefully adapted to cultural contexts. Humor varies widely across cultures—what elicits laughter in one country might fall flat or even offend in another. Research the norms and sense of humor in your audience's region to ensure your approach is appropriate. Tailor anecdotes to reflect their experiences and sensibilities, ensuring they are inclusive and respectful. When in doubt, choose humor centered on universal themes, such as the absurdities of daily life or common human experiences. This approach entertains while building rapport, making your audience more receptive to your message.

Metaphors and Analogies: Bridging Cultural Gaps

Choosing metaphors and analogies that resonate across cultures is another critical aspect of global communication. Metaphors that make sense in one culture may be meaningless—or even confusing—in another. Avoid culturally specific idioms that may not translate well, and instead, use universal themes and symbols. For instance, the concept of a "journey" is universally understood as a path to growth or transformation, and the metaphor of "climbing a mountain" evokes overcoming challenges. These symbols transcend cultural barriers, connecting with audiences on a deeper level. Thoughtfully selected metaphors ensure clarity and foster connection, helping your message resonate universally.

Balancing Global Consistency with Local Adaptation

While engaging global audiences, striking a balance between global consistency and local adaptation is vital. Your core message should remain consistent, reflecting your values and objectives. However, adapting the delivery of this message to fit local nuances demonstrates respect for and understanding of cultural differences. Global brands offer excellent examples of this strategy. For instance, McDonald's maintains its global identity while offering region-specific menu items that cater to local tastes. Similarly, you can tailor your content to address cultural preferences while maintaining the essence of your message. This approach fosters relevance and a sense of belonging among local audiences, enhancing the overall impact of your communication.

Overcoming Language Barriers

Engaging multilingual audiences requires strategies that transform language from a barrier into a tool for connection. Professional translation and interpretation services are invaluable for ensuring your message is conveyed accurately. Simplifying your language—using clear, concise sentences and avoiding jargon or complex terminology—further aids understanding, especially for non-native speakers. Providing translated materials or subtitles enhances accessibility, enabling your audience to engage with your content in their preferred language. These efforts not only improve comprehension but also demonstrate respect for linguistic diversity.

Encouraging Multilingual Dialogue

Fostering multilingual dialogue can enhance audience engagement and inclusivity. Create opportunities for audience participation, such as Q&A sessions or interactive discussions, and offer materials in multiple languages. Digital platforms with automatic translation features can facilitate real-time interaction across language barriers. By incorporating these tools, you show your commitment to inclusivity and respect for your audience's diverse linguistic backgrounds.

7.3 Inclusivity in Language and Content

In today's interconnected world, inclusive language is essential. The words we choose shape perceptions and can either unite or alienate. As you prepare your presentations, ensure your language uplifts and respects everyone. Avoid gender-specific terms by opting for inclusive alternatives. For instance, replace "chairman" with "chairperson" or simply "chair." These small but meaningful changes foster a sense of belonging among all audience members. Person-first language is equally vital. Instead of saying "disabled person," use "person with a disability." This phrasing acknowledges the individual before the condition, emphasizing dignity and respect. By adopting these practices, you create an environment where everyone feels valued and included.

Ensuring content accessibility for diverse audiences is another key aspect of inclusivity. Consider the needs of participants from varied linguistic or cultural backgrounds. Providing translated materials, captions, or subtitles ensures that non-native speakers can fully engage with your message. Designing visually accessible presentations is equally important. Use clear, legible fonts and high-contrast colors to enhance readability. Ensure that visual aids support your spoken content without overwhelming it. Prioritizing accessibility demonstrates your commitment to inclusivity, ensuring all audience members can follow along and contribute meaningfully.

Incorporating diverse perspectives and voices into your content enriches your message and fosters deeper engagement. Drawing on examples from a range of cultural, social, and professional backgrounds provides a more comprehensive understanding of your topic. Sharing stories from different cultures invites your audience to view the world through multiple lenses, encouraging empathy and connection. Citing diverse experts and sources adds credibility and breadth to your narrative, showing that you've considered various viewpoints. This approach not only enhances your presentation's depth but also reflects the diversity of the world we live in, creating an environment for richer discussions and inclusive dialogue.

Creating an Inclusive Environment

Inclusivity extends beyond the content of your presentation—it's about fostering a tone of respect and openness throughout the interaction. Start by establishing ground rules to ensure everyone feels safe and respected. Encourage active listening and open dialogue, making it clear that all voices are welcome and valued. This atmosphere of mutual respect and understanding paves the way for meaningful exchanges and a deeper connection with your audience. Invite feedback and remain open to learning from the experiences and perspectives of others. This reciprocal exchange of ideas not only enriches the conversation but also creates a collaborative and inclusive dynamic. By cultivating an environment where everyone feels heard and appreciated, you enhance audience engagement and create a space for genuine connection.

7.4 Avoiding Common Cultural Missteps

In global communication, assumptions, and stereotypes can under-mine genuine connections. Stereotypes—oversimplified ideas about a group—reduce individuals to labels, disregarding the richness of their unique experiences and backgrounds. These generalizations not only diminish the speaker's credibility but also risk alienating the audience, who may feel misunderstood or undervalued. To foster authentic engagement, approach each interaction with curiosity and sensitivity. Challenge preconceived notions by actively seeking to understand the nuances that define each culture. This mindset fosters respect and opens pathways for meaningful dialogue, turning potential barriers into opportunities for connection.

Navigating cultural taboos and sensitive topics requires a thought-ful balance of preparation and empathy. Each culture has its own taboos—subjects deemed inappropriate or disrespectful to discuss, such as political affiliations, religious beliefs, or specific social norms. Thorough research is essential for identifying these sensitivities and steering clear of topics that might cause discomfort or tension. How-ever, even with the best preparation, missteps can happen. If you unintentionally broach a sensitive topic, remain calm and composed. Acknowledge the situation with empathy and, if necessary, offer a sin-cere apology. This demonstrates respect for your audience's cultural context and creates an atmosphere of trust. By showing a willingness to adapt and learn, you foster open communication and mutual un-derstanding.

Cultural misunderstandings are an inevitable part of intercultural interactions. The key is not to avoid them entirely but to handle them with grace and adaptability. View misunderstandings as opportuni-ties for growth and learning. When they occur, approach the situation with empathy, seeking to understand your audience's perspective. Humor, when used thoughtfully and respectfully, can help diffuse tension and ease discomfort. A quick, genuine apology or clarification can also go a long way in mending the situation. These responses show your audience that you value their perspective and are committed to understanding and respect. By addressing misunderstandings proactively, you not only salvage the interaction but also build trust and strengthen your connection with your audience.

Reflecting on and Learning from Cultural Missteps

Reflecting on past cultural missteps is a vital step toward continuous improvement. Organizations that have faced cultural blunders provide valuable lessons in navigating global communication. Consider a company that launched a campaign well-received in one region but poorly in another due to cultural insensitivity. Analyzing these cases allows you to identify common pitfalls and develop proactive strategies to avoid similar missteps in your own interactions. This reflection should be an ongoing practice, enabling you to adapt and refine your communication style as you gain experience in diverse settings.

Developing a plan for continuous cultural learning is essential for staying attuned to the complexities of global communication. Seek feedback from colleagues and mentors who bring different perspectives. Engage in regular cultural training, attend workshops, or explore literature on cross-cultural communication. These efforts not only deepen your understanding but also demonstrate a commitment to growth and adaptability. By making cultural learning an integral part of your professional development, you position yourself as a communicator who values inclusivity and is prepared for the dynamic nature of global interactions.

In the grand tapestry of global communication, avoiding cultural missteps is not just about sidestepping faux pas—it's about fostering genuine connections built on mutual respect and understanding. By challenging stereotypes, navigating sensitive topics with care, handling misunderstandings with empathy, and committing to lifelong learning, you create an environment where diverse voices are heard, valued, and empowered.

Chapter Eight

Technology Integration

Emerging technologies like virtual and augmented reality are also reshaping how audiences interact with presentations. By experimenting with these tools, speakers can create immersive experiences that go beyond traditional slides and visuals. Such innovations can leave a lasting impact when used thoughtfully.

Picture this: you're in a dimly lit conference room, the hum of a projector in the background. As slides illuminate the screen, your audience shifts in their seats, anticipation mingling with curiosity. This moment is yours. It's an opportunity to not only convey your message but to captivate. In today's digital age, visual aids are no longer optional accessories; they are pivotal tools that can elevate your presentation from mundane to memorable. They transform complex ideas into accessible insights, helping your audience engage and retain information. However, the art lies in using these tools thoughtfully—enhancing your delivery without becoming dependent on them. The key is to let visuals complement your words, not overshadow them.

8.1 Using Visual Aids without Dependency

Visual aids possess the unique ability to clarify complex ideas, making them easier for your audience to grasp.

Infographics, for example, distill vast amounts of data into cohesive, digestible visuals. Imagine presenting quarterly sales figures: rather than overwhelming your audience with a wall of numbers, an infographic can highlight trends, offering a clear and compelling snapshot at a glance. Similarly, diagrams illustrate processes or relationships that might otherwise seem abstract when described verbally. Whether you're explaining a workflow or introducing the mechanics of a new product, diagrams provide clarity and context, bridging the gap between concept and understanding. When used thoughtfully, these tools enhance your message, ensuring it resonates with your audience.

Striking a balance between visual aids and verbal delivery is crucial.

Over-reliance on visuals can detract from your message, turning an engaging presentation into a passive viewing experience. To avoid this, limit the text on your slides to key points that complement your speech. Let your visuals act as prompts that guide your narrative, ensuring the audience's primary focus remains on you, the speaker. This interplay of words and images creates a dynamic, harmonious experience. By maintaining this equilibrium, you capture your audience's attention, keeping them engaged and invested in your message.

Crafting visually appealing and professional slides is a skill that requires careful attention to detail.

Consistency is key. Choose a color scheme and font style that align with your brand, and maintain this design throughout your presentation. Uniformity fosters a sense of professionalism, ensuring your slides enhance rather than distract from your message. Additionally, invest in high-quality images and graphics. Poorly chosen or pixelated visuals can diminish your credibility, while clear, relevant imagery elevates your presentation's impact. Think of your slides as an extension of your message, with every element working to reinforce and resonate.

Minimalistic slide designs are particularly effective for maintaining audience focus.

Strategic use of whitespace can draw attention to key points, making them stand out without competing for attention. A simple visual can convey more than a cluttered one, guiding your audience's gaze to the most important information. Highlight your key points with straightforward visuals that complement your narrative. Research has shown that people retain information better when it's presented alongside relevant images. By embracing minimalism, you create a clean, focused presentation that keeps your audience engaged.

When used effectively, visual aids have the power to transform a presentation, making it engaging, memorable, and impactful.

They simplify complex concepts, enhance verbal delivery, and reinforce professionalism. By balancing visuals with words, crafting appealing slides, and adopting a minimalist approach, you ensure your message leaves a lasting impression.

Reflection Exercise

Review a recent presentation you delivered and evaluate your slides. Consider how they supported—or detracted from—your verbal delivery. Did they enhance your message or overshadow it? Reflect on ways to refine your visual aids to create a more balanced and harmonious presentation. Focus on the principles of consistency, simplicity, and engagement as you assess your approach.

8.2 Interactive Apps for Audience Participation

Engaging an audience is often the cornerstone of a successful presentation.

In today's digital age, interactive apps have transformed the way we connect with listeners, offering dynamic tools to gauge understanding and foster meaningful exchanges. Platforms like Slido and Mentimeter empower presenters by turning a one-way speech into a two-way conversation. Imagine pausing mid-presentation to assess how well your audience grasps a concept. With live polls, you can not only gauge understanding but also invite active participation. This real-time feedback is invaluable, enabling you to adjust your delivery on the spot to ensure clarity and engagement. It also empowers your audience, making them feel like active participants rather than passive listeners.

Interactive Q&A sessions are another effective way to encourage engagement.

Apps designed for this purpose streamline the process by organizing and prioritizing questions, reducing the potential chaos of live discussions. Participants can submit questions anonymously, creating a safe space for those who might feel hesitant to speak up. This anonymity often leads to a more diverse range of questions, enriching the conversation. By structuring the flow of questions, these apps ensure the session remains focused and productive. Addressing each query thoughtfully demonstrates your attentiveness and adaptability—qualities that resonate strongly with any audience. This approach transforms a traditional presentation into a collaborative dialogue, fostering a sense of community and shared learning.

Gamification is a powerful tool to captivate your audience's attention and make learning enjoyable.

Quiz apps, for example, allow you to test knowledge in a fun, interactive manner, injecting energy and a sense of friendly competition into the room. For decision-making scenarios, interactive storytelling apps offer platforms where audiences can explore different outcomes based on their choices. This active participation reinforces learning while encouraging critical thinking. As attendees engage with these gamified elements, they transition from passive observers to active contributors, enhancing both their retention of information and enjoyment of the presentation. Storytelling serves as the bridge between facts and emotions, allowing the audience to visualize and internalize the message. Adding a vivid description or a relatable personal anecdote can make the message even more memorable. Think of a moment when a story changed your perspective—it is this transformation that storytelling brings to public speaking.

For diverse audiences, accessibility is paramount, and technology provides innovative solutions.

Real-time translation apps help eliminate language barriers by translating spoken words into the audience's preferred language. Captioning services for live presentations cater to individuals who are deaf or hard of hearing, ensuring everyone can fully engage with the content. These tools demonstrate a commitment to inclusivity, fostering an environment where every participant feels valued. By incorporating such technologies, you not only broaden your reach but also ensure that your message resonates across linguistic and physical boundaries. Emerging technologies like virtual and augmented reality are also reshaping how audiences interact with presentations. By experimenting with these tools, speakers can create immersive experiences that go beyond traditional slides and visuals. Such innovations can leave a lasting impact when used thoughtfully.

Interactive apps go beyond adding flair to a presentation; they fundamentally enhance engagement and understanding.

They transform traditional speeches into dynamic experiences that resonate with a wide array of audiences. Whether through live polls, structured Q&A sessions, gamification, or accessibility tools, these technologies enable you to connect with your audience on a deeper level. This connection fosters a more interactive, inclusive, and memorable experience, leaving a lasting impression on your listeners and amplifying the impact of your message.

8.3 Virtual Reality and Augmented Reality in Presentations

Imagine stepping into a room where the boundaries of reality blur, and your audience is transported into a world where they can interact with your ideas firsthand. This isn't a scene from a science fiction novel—it's the transformative potential of Virtual Reality (VR) and Augmented Reality (AR) in modern presentations. With VR headsets, you can offer your audience a fully immersive experience, such as a virtual tour of your latest architectural project, where every intricate detail is visible and tangible. Imagine walking clients through a digital landscape, showing them how each component fits into the broader vision. This level of immersion offers a depth of understanding that words, diagrams, or static images can never achieve, transforming passive listeners into active participants.

AR takes interactivity to a whole new level by overlaying digital elements in the real world.

Picture conducting a product demonstration where attendees use their devices to see interactive features appear on the actual product in front of them. A simple point of a smartphone camera could reveal pop-up animations detailing the benefits of a new software tool or even step-by-step guides to using it. By blending reality with dynamic enhancements, AR turns abstract concepts into hands-on experiences. These moments not only captivate attention but also deepen retention, making your message memorable long after your presentation ends.

Designing Engaging VR and AR Content

Creating VR and AR content that educates and captivates requires more than just technical prowess—it demands thoughtful design and relevance. Interactive 3D models can provide your audience with a tangible way to explore ideas. Imagine a virtual workshop where participants can examine and manipulate a model engine, disassembling and reassembling its parts to understand its mechanics. Similarly, immersive environments enable experiential learning, such as virtual scenarios for crisis management training or simulations of bustling markets for sales professionals to hone their pitches. These scenarios shift learning from passive consumption to active engagement, bridging the gap between theory and practice.

The key is to ensure that VR and AR content aligns seamlessly with your objectives. Each experience should serve a clear purpose, whether it's simplifying complex ideas, encouraging hands-on exploration, or fostering critical thinking. By prioritizing content relevance and interactivity, you enhance the audience's learning experience without overwhelming or distracting them.

Seamless Integration into Presentations

For VR and AR to enhance your message, integration must feel natural and unobtrusive. Transitions between real-world and virtual elements should be smooth to maintain focus and avoid disorientation. For instance, if you're moving from a traditional slide deck to an immersive VR experience, guide your audience with clear instructions and context. Pre-recorded VR demonstrations can be a valuable tool for maintaining narrative control and ensuring that technical glitches don't derail your message. Similarly, AR demonstrations should be intuitive and easy for your audience to access, whether through smartphones, tablets, or AR glasses. Properly rehearsing these transitions ensures a cohesive experience, keeping the focus on your message rather than the technology itself. Emerging technologies like virtual and augmented reality are also reshaping how audiences interact with presentations. By experimenting with these tools, speakers can create immersive experiences that go beyond traditional slides and visuals. Such innovations can leave a lasting impact when used thoughtfully.

Evaluating the Impact of VR and AR

The true measure of VR and AR's success lies in their ability to enhance understanding and engagement. Collect feedback from your audience to determine how these tools resonate. Did the VR tour help clarify complex concepts? Did the AR overlay spark new questions or inspire deeper insights? Post-presentation evaluations can include audience surveys, retention tests, or informal discussions to gauge how effectively the technology supported your objectives. Emerging technologies like virtual and augmented reality are also reshaping how audiences interact with presentations. By experimenting with these tools, speakers can create immersive experiences that go beyond traditional slides and visuals. Such innovations can leave a lasting impact when used thoughtfully.

Additionally, track metrics such as retention rates and post-event applications of the knowledge shared. If participants are recalling and applying the lessons learned during your presentation, it's a strong indication that VR and AR played a valuable role. These insights help refine your approach, ensuring that future presentations are even more impactful.

Transforming Presentations with VR and AR

VR and AR are no longer futuristic novelties—they are tools that can redefine how we communicate ideas and engage audiences. By integrating these technologies, you transform your presentations into immersive experiences that resonate on multiple sensory levels. Whether you're walking clients through a virtual project, guiding your team through an augmented workflow, or providing interactive learning environments, these tools amplify your message's reach and impact.

Explore VR and AR not as mere enhancements but as integral parts of your storytelling strategy. By combining their immersive power with thoughtful content and seamless integration, you create presentations that educate, captivate, and inspire. As you embrace these innovations, you position yourself at the forefront of communication, offering experiences that are as unforgettable as they are effective. Storytelling serves as the bridge between facts and emotions, allowing the audience to visualize and internalize the message. Adding a vivid description or a relatable personal anecdote can make the message even more memorable. Think of a moment when a story changed your perspective—it is this transformation that storytelling brings to public speaking.

Chapter Nine

Emotional Intelligence

In the world of public speaking, the ability to read and respond to your audience sets great speakers apart. Imagine yourself standing before a sea of faces, each carrying its own set of emotions and expectations. The pressure is palpable, yet within this challenge lies an opportunity to connect deeply. Emotional intelligence, or EQ, is your compass in this landscape. It guides you not only to deliver your message but to truly resonate with your audience. This chapter delves into the nuanced art of understanding audience emotions and adjusting your delivery to create a profound impact.

9.1 Recognizing Audience Emotions

Understanding audience emotions begins with recognizing the subtle cues that reveal their emotional state. **Facial expressions** serve as windows into the audience's mind. A slight furrow of the brow might indicate confusion, while a nod accompanied by a smile suggests agreement and engagement. **Body language** offers further clues: leaning in often signifies interest, while crossed arms can signal defensiveness or disengagement.

Listen carefully for **tone and vocal inflections** within the room. A collective sigh might indicate relief or understanding, whereas hushed murmurs could suggest confusion or disagreement. These auditory signals, paired with visual observations, help you construct a comprehensive picture of the audience's emotional landscape.

Beyond individual cues, take note of the **overall mood and group dynamics**. Are they buzzing with energy, eagerly awaiting your next point? Or are they subdued, perhaps overwhelmed by the information? Spotting signs of **interest or boredom** is critical. A room filled with attentive gazes and active participation speaks of engagement while fidgeting and distracted glances signal waning attention. Recognizing group consensus or division can also guide your approach: a unified audience may respond well to collective affirmations, while a divided one might require addressing differing perspectives with sensitivity.

Adjusting Delivery to Match Emotions

Adjusting your delivery based on audience emotions is where your adaptability shines. **Tone and pace** play pivotal roles. If you sense excitement in the room, match it with an energetic delivery, using varied intonation to maintain enthusiasm. On the other hand, if the atmosphere feels tense, slow down and speak with clarity, cultivating a sense of calm and understanding.

Adapt the **emphasis of your content** to the audience's mood. If a particular story visibly moves your audience, take the opportunity to expand on it, building on the emotional connection. Conversely, if the audience seems overwhelmed, simplify and clarify your message to ensure accessibility. Flexibility in your delivery ensures that your message not only reaches your audience but resonates deeply.

Anticipating Audience Reactions

Utilizing emotional intelligence to anticipate audience reactions transforms a good presentation into a great one. Consider **potential objections or challenges** your content might provoke and prepare empathetic responses. For example, if you're discussing a contentious topic, acknowledge differing viewpoints upfront to build trust and rapport. By predicting the **emotional triggers** your message might evoke, you can frame your content in ways that inspire understanding and action.

Guide your audience's emotional journey by **navigating their responses thoughtfully**. If your message addresses a pain point, balance empathy with actionable solutions to uplift and empower them. When presenting an inspiring vision, use vivid storytelling and affirmative language to spark motivation. Emotional intelligence allows you to craft a presentation that not only informs but also moves your audience, leaving a lasting impression. Storytelling serves as the bridge between facts and emotions, allowing the audience to visualize and internalize the message. Adding a vivid description or a relatable personal anecdote can make the message even more memorable. Think of a moment when a story changed your perspective—it is this transformation that storytelling brings to public speaking.

Reflection Exercise: Building EQ for Public Speaking

After your next presentation, reflect on the audience's emotional responses. What cues did you observe? Were there moments when engagement heightened or waned? How did you adjust your delivery to align with their emotions? Use this reflection to identify areas for growth, enhancing your ability to read and respond effectively to diverse audiences.

By honing your emotional intelligence, you elevate your ability to connect with your audience on a profound level. Recognizing emotional cues, adapting your delivery, and anticipating reactions are skills that enable you to resonate beyond words. Emotional intelligence transforms a presentation into an experience—one that informs, inspires, and leaves a lasting impact.

9.2 Adapting Your Delivery Based on Audience Feedback

Imagine standing before an audience, the spotlight warm on your face and a sea of eyes focused intently on you. In these moments, the real-time feedback you receive becomes invaluable—a compass guiding your presentation, showing when you've struck the right chord or when adjustments are needed. Encouraging **questions and comments** throughout your presentation transform a monologue into a dynamic conversation. By inviting your audience to engage, you gain insights into their thoughts and reactions. Leveraging **live polling tools,** such as Slido or Mentimeter, offers another way to gather instant feedback. These tools allow participants to share their opinions or questions anonymously, encouraging even the most reserved individuals to participate. The immediate results provide a snapshot of the room's collective mindset, helping you adjust your course in real time.

Reading and Responding to Feedback Cues

Adapting to real-time feedback requires both attentiveness and flexibility. Observe subtle shifts in audience demeanor as you speak. Are they **leaning forward**, showing interest, or **glancing at their phones**, signaling disengagement? These cues reveal whether your message resonates or if adjustments are necessary.

If engagement wanes, adapt by altering your delivery style. Consider injecting a relevant **story or example** to rekindle interest. Responding to unscripted **questions from the audience** is another valuable skill to master. These inquiries often reflect genuine curiosity or confusion, presenting opportunities to clarify or expand on your points. Addressing questions with thoughtfulness and confidence not only demonstrates your expertise but also builds rapport and fosters a sense of collaboration within the room. True confidence is built through both preparation and stepping outside your comfort zone. By integrating these techniques into your routine, you build long-term confidence.

Maintaining Flexibility in Delivery

Flexibility is crucial for sustaining engagement. While preparation is key, your ability to adapt in the moment can elevate your presentation. Striking a balance between planned content and spontaneous interactions creates a dynamic, responsive delivery.

For example:

- If your audience expresses **enthusiasm for a particular topic**, delve deeper, even if it wasn't part of your original plan.

- Conversely, if a segment doesn't resonate, be ready to **move on swiftly** to maintain energy and focus.

- Tailor the depth of your content to your audience's knowledge level. A well-informed group may appreciate a **technical deep dive**, while a general audience may benefit from **broad concepts and relatable examples**.

This adaptability ensures that your presentation remains relevant and impactful, no matter the audience's expertise or interests.

Reflecting on Feedback for Future Growth

Reflection after a presentation is an essential step in refining your skills. Take time to review **feedback forms, comments, and audience reactions**. These insights often highlight strengths to build upon and areas for improvement. Look for patterns in the feedback—are there recurring questions or criticisms? These trends pinpoint aspects of your presentation that may require adjustment.

Incorporate this feedback into your preparation for future presentations. For example:

- If multiple participants request more **real-world examples**, expand on practical applications in your next session.

- If feedback indicates that a certain **section felt rushed**, consider pacing adjustments during rehearsals.

This ongoing process of reflection and adaptation sharpens your skills and demonstrates to your audience that you value their input.

Incorporating Feedback into Practice

Developing a habit of reflecting on audience feedback involves humility and a willingness to grow. Consider keeping a **post-presentation journal** where you document moments of connection, areas of disengagement, and key takeaways. For instance:

- What sections elicited the most **engagement** or **questions**?

- Were there moments where the audience seemed **confused or distracted**?

Use these observations to refine your approach, cultivating a mindset of curiosity and openness.

By consistently analyzing and integrating feedback, you evolve into a more effective and confident communicator. This commitment to growth enhances your ability to adapt in real-time and strengthens your connection with your audience, as they see you actively working to provide an engaging and meaningful experience.

Through the continuous practice of gathering, analyzing, and applying feedback, you transform presentations into opportunities for connection and learning. Audience feedback becomes not just a tool for improvement but a bridge to deeper engagement, ensuring your message resonates with authenticity and impact.

9.3 Building Empathy Through Stories

Stories hold immense power in bridging the gap between the speaker and the audience. By crafting narratives that resonate emotionally, you can create an environment where empathy flourishes. Focus on shared experiences and universal themes that your audience can relate to. Whether it's the challenge of overcoming adversity or the joy of achieving a hard-earned goal, these common threads weave a tapestry of connection. Highlighting struggles and triumphs humanizes you, transforming the presentation from a monologue to a shared experience. When you delve into narratives that mirror your audience's experiences, you invite them to walk alongside you, sharing in your journey.

Personal anecdotes are your key to fostering empathy and building trust. Sharing stories that reveal personal challenges and growth fosters a sense of honesty and vulnerability. When you open up about your own struggles, you show that you're relatable, that you've faced hurdles and emerged stronger. This openness breaks down barriers, inviting your audience to see you as more than just a speaker; you're a fellow traveler on the path of life. Connecting your personal experiences to audience situations is a powerful way to engender empathy. Perhaps you've faced a similar challenge to one your audience is grappling with. Share how you navigated that situation, the lessons you learned, and how you grew from it. This connection not only builds rapport but also positions you as a source of insight and encouragement.

Balancing vulnerability and professionalism is a delicate dance. While sharing personal stories can be impactful, it's crucial to assess the appropriateness of your disclosures. Consider the context and the audience's expectations. Sharing too much can shift the focus from the message to the messenger, potentially overshadowing your core points. Keep the focus on the message you want to convey, ensuring that your personal anecdotes serve to enhance, rather than distract from, your main message. By maintaining a professional demeanor throughout, you reinforce the credibility of your narrative.

Encouraging audience empathy through relatable narratives is about inviting them to step into the shoes of your story. Use vivid imagery to create emotional immersion. Paint a picture with words, allowing your audience to envision the scene, feel the emotions, and experience the journey with you. This sensory engagement draws them in, making the story not just yours but theirs, too. Inviting audience reflection and discussion further deepens this connection. Pose questions that encourage them to think about how the story's themes apply to their own lives. Create space for discussion, allowing them to share their perspectives and insights. This interaction transforms a one-way narrative into a shared exploration.

Incorporate these strategies to elevate your narratives, turning them into powerful tools of connection and empathy. When your stories resonate, your audience is more likely to engage, reflect, and remember. They walk away not just with information but with a sense of connection and understanding that lingers long after the presentation ends.

***

9.4 The Power of Active Listening in Speaking

Active listening might seem like a straightforward skill, yet its impact on public speaking is profound. When you're in front of an audience, maintaining **eye contact** is more than a courtesy; it's a bridge that connects you to your listeners. This simple act assures them that their presence matters, fostering a sense of engagement. **Your posture** also plays a pivotal role. Standing tall and facing your audience signals confidence and openness, inviting them to reciprocate with attention and interest. As you nod or offer verbal affirmations like "I see" or "That's interesting," you show that you're tuned into their reactions. These gestures, while small, transform passive listeners into active participants. By practicing active listening, you create a **dialogue** rather than a monologue, turning your presentation into a shared experience.

Integrating Audience Input for Enhanced Engagement

Integrating **audience input** into your presentation is a dynamic way to enhance engagement and relevance. When an audience member shares an insight or raises a question, acknowledge their contribution with sincerity. For example, saying, *"That's a great point,"* and weaving their input into your narrative validates their perspective, enhancing the collaborative atmosphere. Building on audience questions or suggestions not only enriches your presentation but also demonstrates your **adaptability**.

If someone asks a question that aligns with your topic, expand on it and use it as a stepping stone to delve deeper into your subject. This approach helps you cater to the audience's curiosity, keeping them engaged and invested in the discourse. Incorporating these moments into your delivery allows your presentation to evolve naturally, fostering a sense of shared ownership between you and your listeners.

Reflecting and Paraphrasing for Clarity and Trust

Reflecting and paraphrasing audience feedback is crucial for ensuring clarity and mutual understanding. When someone shares a thought or raises a concern, take a moment to summarize their point with a phrase like, *"So, what I hear you saying is..."* This technique not only clarifies the discussion but also validates their emotions and perspectives.

Reflecting their words back to them shows respect and appreciation for their input, solidifying **trust**. This practice turns a simple exchange into a meaningful dialogue where both parties feel heard and valued. It's not just about responding to their words but also acknowledging the emotions and thoughts behind them, fostering a deeper connection.

Active Listening as a Tool for Credibility and Trust

Using active listening enhances both your **credibility** and trustworthiness. When you actively listen, you demonstrate that you value and respect your audience's input. This respect is reciprocated, fostering an inclusive atmosphere where listeners feel safe and appreciated.

This **trust** encourages openness and engagement, making your audience more likely to share their thoughts, ask questions, and fully immerse themselves in the presentation. By cultivating this atmosphere, you transform your speaking engagements into shared journeys of discovery and understanding. Your audience views you as a partner in the conversation, strengthening their connection to both you and your message.

Active Listening as a Transformative Approach

Active listening is more than a skill; it's a transformative approach that elevates public speaking from a one-sided speech to a dynamic **dialogue**. Through **eye contact, posture, and verbal affirmations**, you connect with your audience, making them feel seen and heard. Incorporating their input enriches the discussion while reflecting and paraphrasing their feedback ensures clarity and mutual understanding.

These practices not only enhance your credibility but also foster **trust and collaboration**, turning your presentations into meaningful and impactful experiences. As you continue to refine your active listening skills, you'll find your ability to engage and connect with your audience deepens, making each speaking opportunity more rewarding and successful.

Closing Reflection on Emotional Intelligence in Public Speaking

In this chapter, we explored the power of **emotional intelligence** in enhancing public speaking. You can create more engaging and impactful presentations by understanding audience emotions, adapting your delivery based on feedback, building empathy through stories, and practicing active listening. These insights emphasize the importance of connecting with your audience on an emotional level.

As we move into the next chapter, we'll focus on the significance of **preparation and practice**, uncovering strategies for mastering public speaking and ensuring that every presentation leaves a lasting impression.

Chapter Ten

Continuous Improvement and Mastery

Imagine standing on the threshold of a grand journey, where every step builds upon the last, leading you toward a landscape of confidence and eloquence. Public speaking isn't just an art; it's a dynamic process of growth and self-discovery. Like any skill, it demands dedication and a structured approach. The path to mastery is lined with goals that guide you, milestones that celebrate your progress, and challenges that test your resolve. This chapter will illuminate how setting and achieving goals can transform your public speaking abilities, turning fear into fuel for growth.

10.1 Setting and Achieving Speaking Goals

The journey to becoming a skilled speaker begins with setting clear and measurable goals. These goals act as your roadmap, guiding you through the intricate paths of public speaking development. The SMART criteria—an acronym for Specific, Measurable, Achievable, Relevant, and Time-bound—provides a framework to ensure these goals are effective:

- **Specific**: Pinpoint exactly what you aim to achieve, such as delivering a compelling speech in a particular setting.

- **Measurable**: Define how you will assess progress, such as audience engagement, self-evaluation, or feedback.

- **Achievable**: Set goals that stretch your abilities while remaining realistic to avoid frustration.

- **Relevant**: Align your goals with your broader life, career, or educational objectives.

- **Time-bound**: Establish clear deadlines, creating urgency and focus.

This structured approach enhances motivation and self-esteem, propelling you forward in your speaking journey.

Breaking Down Goals into Actionable Steps

Once you've set your goals, breaking them down into actionable steps transforms overwhelming ambitions into manageable tasks. Creating a step-by-step action plan allows you to visualize the path clearly, identifying each necessary task. Prioritize tasks based on importance and urgency, ensuring your efforts focus where they matter most.

For instance, if your goal is to deliver a TED-style talk, break it down into steps such as selecting your topic, researching your audience, crafting your narrative, and rehearsing your delivery. Each completed task fosters a sense of accomplishment, turning the climb toward success into a series of achievable milestones. This process makes the journey less daunting and encourages steady, measurable progress.

Tracking Progress and Maintaining Alignment

Tracking your progress is essential for staying aligned with your objectives and allows room for adjustment as needed. Consider maintaining a growth journal to document your goals, track your progress, and reflect on lessons learned after each presentation. This practice not only reinforces a growth mindset but also creates a tangible record of your journey.

Goal-setting apps can further streamline this process, offering reminders and insights to keep you on track. For example, you can set daily or weekly check-ins to evaluate your progress. Regularly reviewing and updating your goals ensures they remain relevant and challenging, pushing you to refine and expand your public speaking skills continually.

Overcoming Obstacles and Building Resilience

Pursuing ambitious goals often means encountering obstacles along the way. Addressing these challenges directly is essential for maintaining momentum. Common hurdles include:

- **Procrastination and Time Management Issues**: Combat these by setting clear priorities and adhering to your action plan. Break tasks into smaller, time-bound segments to avoid overwhelm.

- **Self-Doubt or Fear of Failure**: Replace negative self-talk with affirmations, focusing on the progress you've made rather than perfection.

- **Plateaus in Improvement**: When progress slows, reassess your strategies and seek external feedback to identify new areas for growth.

Building resilience and perseverance is equally critical. Remind yourself that setbacks are part of the journey, not the end. Every challenge provides an opportunity to learn and grow, reinforcing your resolve and sharpening your skills. By reframing obstacles as stepping stones, you cultivate the determination to keep moving forward, even when the path is steep.

Reflection Exercise: Progress Mapping

Reflect on a recent speaking goal you set for yourself. Did you use the SMART framework? How did you break the goal into steps, and what challenges did you encounter? Take a moment to write down what worked well and what could be improved. Use this reflection to refine your approach to future goals, ensuring continuous growth and alignment with your vision.

10.2 Joining Communities for Ongoing Support

Why Community Matters

Public speaking can sometimes feel like a solitary journey, but it doesn't have to be. Surrounding yourself with a supportive community accelerates your growth and provides invaluable feedback and encouragement. These communities foster a sense of camaraderie and shared purpose, transforming your journey into a collective effort.

Formal Organizations

- **Toastmasters International**: As one of the most recognized public speaking organizations, Toastmasters provides a structured environment where you can practice and receive constructive feedback. Its programs focus on both speaking skills and leadership development, offering a well-rounded approach.

- **Local Speaking Clubs**: Seek out smaller, locally organized speaking groups that might cater to specific niches or interests. These intimate settings often provide personalized feedback and a supportive network.

Online Forums and Social Media Groups

Digital platforms connect you with a global audience of like-minded speakers:

- **Online Forums**: Participate in discussions on platforms like Reddit's public speaking communities or specialized forums dedicated to communication skills.

- **Social Media Groups**: Join LinkedIn or Facebook groups

for speakers, where members share tips, resources, and inspiration. These spaces often host virtual events or challenges that keep you motivated and engaged.

By engaging in these communities, you gain access to a wealth of diverse experiences and perspectives, enriching your understanding and approach.

Active Participation for Maximum Benefit

Active involvement in community activities transforms passive learning into dynamic growth:

- **Workshops and Meetings**: Attend regular events to observe others, practice your skills, and absorb new techniques. These sessions are designed to create a safe environment for experimentation and feedback.

- **Volunteering Opportunities**: Take on speaking roles within the group, such as leading a discussion or presenting on a topic. This hands-on experience reinforces your confidence and skills.

Proactive engagement creates a cycle of learning and sharing, where you contribute to the community while simultaneously enhancing your abilities.

Building a Network of Mentors and Peers

A strong network of mentors and peers is essential for sustained growth:

- **Mentors**: Seek out individuals who inspire you and align with your goals. Mentors offer tailored advice, helping you navigate challenges and refine your skills.

- **Peer Support**: Connect with fellow speakers who are at a similar stage in their journey. Sharing feedback and celebrating each other's milestones creates accountability and motivation.

These relationships form the backbone of your speaking journey, offering guidance, encouragement, and collaboration.

Leveraging Community Resources

Communities often provide extensive resources to help you grow:

- **Educational Tools**: Access workshops, webinars, and curated reading lists that deepen your understanding of public speaking techniques.

- **Group Challenges**: Participate in exercises that push you out of your comfort zone, such as impromptu speaking sessions or storytelling challenges.

- **Feedback Opportunities**: Regularly seek and provide constructive feedback, sharpening your skills through mutual learning.

By fully utilizing these resources, you ensure continuous improvement and stay motivated to reach new heights in your speaking journey.

10.3 Staying Updated with Public Speaking Trends

Keeping Up with Trends

The field of public speaking evolves continuously, shaped by technological advancements and changing audience expectations. Staying informed about current trends ensures you maintain a competitive edge and adapt to the dynamic communication landscape.

- **Follow Thought Leaders**: Subscribe to newsletters, blogs, and podcasts that explore the latest in public speaking techniques. These resources often feature insights from experienced speakers and highlight emerging practices that can inspire your presentations.

- **Stay Curious**: Platforms like LinkedIn and Twitter are valuable for real-time updates on industry innovations and discourse. Engaging with these platforms helps you remain informed and connected.

Integrating Trends into Your Style

New trends, when thoughtfully incorporated, can elevate your presentations and enhance audience engagement.

- **Leverage Virtual and Hybrid Tools**: Experiment with live polls, interactive Q&A sessions, or breakout rooms for online and hybrid settings. These tools foster dialogue and inclusivity, even in remote environments.

- **Experiment with Storytelling Techniques**: Incorporate multimedia storytelling or audience-driven narratives to create immersive experiences. These trends make your presentations more engaging and memorable.

The key is to maintain a balance—enhancing your message without letting technology or gimmicks overshadow your content.

Evaluating and Selecting Trends

Not every trend is worth adopting. Thoughtfully assess each one's relevance to your objectives and audience.

- **Align with Goals**: Consider whether a trend complements your message and resonates with your audience. For instance, using humor or interactive elements might suit a casual seminar but not a formal keynote.

- **Focus on Impact**: Prioritize trends that enhance understanding and engagement without overcomplicating the presentation.

Participating in Trend Discussions

Engaging in discussions about trends helps you deepen your knowledge and establish thought leadership.

- **Share Your Insights**: Write articles, create social media posts, or join webinars to contribute your perspective. Sharing your experiences positions you as an informed and proactive communicator.

- **Connect with Peers**: Engaging with others fosters idea exchange, keeping your approach fresh and innovative.

Interactive Exercise: Trend Exploration

- **Choose a Trend**: Select a current trend in public speaking that interests you.

- **Research Its Application**: Investigate how it's being used and its impact on audiences.

- **Write and Share**: Compose a short article or blog post sharing your findings and ideas for incorporating the trend into your presentations.

- **Seek Feedback**: Share your article in a community or online group to gather insights and perspectives.

Conclusion

Mastery in public speaking is not a final destination but an ongoing journey of growth and discovery. It's about setting ambitious yet attainable goals, embracing the support of a community, and staying informed about the evolving landscape of communication. Each step you take builds on the last, deepening your skills and broadening your impact.

As you continue this journey, remember that growth happens in moments of challenge and triumph alike. Celebrate your progress, however small, and reflect on the lessons learned along the way. By embracing resilience, adaptability, and lifelong learning, you equip yourself to inspire and connect with diverse audiences.

The world is waiting to hear your voice. Take each opportunity with confidence, determination, and authenticity. Public speaking is not just about delivering words—it's about leaving a lasting impression that inspires change and fosters connection.

Final Note of Gratitude

I want to thank you for allowing me to guide you on this transformative journey. Your commitment to improving your public speaking skills is both admirable and inspiring. Each step reflects your dedication to growth and excellence.

Remember, you are not alone. With the support of your peers, mentors, and communities, you can continue to refine your craft and achieve greatness. Embrace every opportunity to speak with confidence and determination, knowing that your voice has the power to inspire and influence.

It has been my honor to be part of your story. Keep speaking, growing, and inspiring. The world is waiting to hear what you have to say.

A note from the Author

Dear Reader,

Thank you for joining me on this journey to mastering public speaking. Writing this book has been one of the most fulfilling challenges of my life because I know how deeply the fear of speaking can hold us back.

For years, I struggled with the same nervousness, doubts, and overthinking that you might be facing. There were moments when I doubted if I'd ever be able to share my thoughts confidently in front of others. But I learned that fear doesn't have to hold us back—it can fuel our growth.

I poured my heart into this book to give you tools that are practical, relatable, and, most importantly, empowering. Whether you're speaking at work, at an event, or simply trying to express yourself more confidently, I hope this book has given you the courage to embrace your voice and share your story.

If you've found value in these pages, it would mean the world to me if you shared your thoughts with others. Your review can help someone else, just like you, discover this book and start their own journey to confidence.

Here's a quick link to leave a review:
https://www.amazon.com/review/review-your-purchases/?asin=B
OOKASIN

Your feedback not only helps others but also motivates me to keep creating resources to help people like you achieve their goals.

Remember, your voice matters, and the world needs to hear it.

With gratitude,
Sawsan Charif

References

- Dr. Alan Jacobson. (n.d.). **CBT for fear of public speaking.** 0

  - Retrieved from https://dralanjacobson.com/cbt-for-fear-of-public-speaking/

- Ethos3. (n.d.). **The benefits of good presentation storytelling.**

  - Retrieved from https://ethos3.com/the-benefits-of-good-presentation-storytelling/

- Everyday Speech. (n.d.). **Empathy: A cornerstone of effective communication and connection.** Retrieved from

  - https://everydayspeech.com/sel-implementation/empathy-a-cornerstone-of-effective-communication-and-connection/

- Future Visual. (n.d.). **Using VR for company presentations.** Retrieved from

  - https://www.futurevisual.com/blog/virtual-reality-company-presentations/

- Hansen, J. (n.d.). **Don't panic! Mastering technical issues in virtual presentations**. Retrieved from

  - https://juliehansen.live/dont-panic-mastering-technical -issues-in-virtual-presentations/

- Harvard Business Review. (2008, November). **How to become an authentic speaker**. Retrieved from

  - https://hbr.org/2008/11/how-to-become-an-authentic -speaker

- Harvard Business Review. (2022, March). **Don't underestimate the power of self-reflection**. Retrieved from

  - https://hbr.org/2022/03/dont-underestimate-the-pow er-of-self-reflection

- Harvard Business Publishing. (n.d.). **The science behind the art of storytelling**. Retrieved from

  - https://www.harvardbusiness.org/the-science-behind-t he-art-of-storytelling/

- Kahoot!. (n.d.). **Interactive presentation tools for business**. Retrieved from

  - https://kahoot.com/business/use-cases/presentations -meetings/

- Language Intelligence. (n.d.). **Global brands that nailed localization in different markets**. Retrieved from

  - https://www.languageintelligence.com/post/global-bra

nds-that-nailed-localization-in-different-markets

- LinkedIn. (n.d.). **6 confidence-building exercises for presentations and public speaking**. Retrieved from

  - https://www.linkedin.com/advice/3/what-some-confidence-building-exercises-you-can

- LinkedIn. (n.d.). **Conquering fear through visualization**. Retrieved from

  - https://www.linkedin.com/pulse/conquering-fear-through-visualization-estra

- LinkedIn. (n.d.). **Empathy and storytelling: How to lead with presentations**. Retrieved from

  - https://www.linkedin.com/advice/0/how-do-you-leverage-empathy-storytelling

- LinkedIn. (n.d.). **How to read and respond to audience body language**. Retrieved from

  - https://www.linkedin.com/advice/0/how-do-you-read-respond-body-language-your

- MasterClass. (n.d.). **Learn about narrative arcs: Definition, examples, and how to create one**. Retrieved from

  - https://www.masterclass.com/articles/what-are-the-elements-of-a-narrative-arc-and-how-do-you-create-one-in-writing

- Medium. (n.d.). **Sensory writing: Engaging all five senses**

for immersive storytelling. Retrieved from

- https://medium.com/@wilbur.greene/sensory-writing -engaging-all-five-senses-for-immersive-storytelling-d3c 96ce51c00

- MindTools. (n.d.). **Active listening: Tips, skills, techniques, and examples**. Retrieved from

    - https://www.mindtools.com/az4wxv7/active-listening

- Pam Terry. (n.d.). **Improv techniques to improve public speaking skills**. Retrieved from https://pamterry.com/im prov-techniques-improve-public-speaking-skills/

- PositivePsychology.com. (n.d.). **How to use mindfulness therapy for anxiety: 15 exercises**. Retrieved from

    - https://positivepsychology.com/mindfulness-for-anxiet y/

- Psychology Today. (2017, June). **Non-verbal communication across cultures**. Retrieved from

    - https://www.psychologytoday.com/us/blog/between-c ultures/201706/non-verbal-communication-across-cult ures

- QuestionPro. (n.d.). **Audience research: What it is, methods + how to conduct it**. Retrieved from

    - https://www.questionpro.com/blog/audience-research /

- Rcademy. (n.d.). **The power of visual aids in enhancing communication**. Retrieved from

  - https://rcademy.com/the-power-of-visual-aids-in-enhancing-communication/

- Systeme.io. (n.d.). **Creating SMART public speaking goals**. Retrieved from

  - https://virtualorator.com/blog/creating-smart-public-speaking-goals/

- Toastmasters International. (n.d.). **The benefits of Toastmasters membership**. Retrieved from

  - https://www.toastmasters.org/resources/the-benefits-of-toastmasters-membership

- Verywell Mind. (2024). **Best time management apps of 2024**. Retrieved from

  - https://www.verywellmind.com/best-time-management-apps-5116817

- Wikipedia. (n.d.). **Power posing**. Retrieved from

  - https://en.wikipedia.org/wiki/Power_posing

- Words Fresh. (n.d.). **How to simplify a complex topic for non-experts**. Retrieved from

  - https://www.wordsfresh.com/how-to-simplify-a-complex-topic-for-non-experts/

www.ingramcontent.com/pod-product-compliance
Lightning Source LLC
Chambersburg PA
CBHW021158130626
46554CB00005B/1871